I0691048

Shulamit Almog
The Origins of the Law in Homer

Law & Literature

Edited by
Daniela Carpi and Klaus Stierstorfer

Volume 21

Shulamit Almog

The Origins of the Law in Homer

—

DE GRUYTER

ISBN 978-3-11-135795-9
e-ISBN (PDF) 978-3-11-076611-0
e-ISBN (EPUB) 978-3-11-076617-2
ISSN 2191-8457

Library of Congress Control Number: 2021951248

Bibliographic information published by the Deutsche Nationalbibliothek
The Deutsche Nationalbibliothek lists this publication in the Deutsche Nationalbibliografie;
detailed bibliographic data are available on the Internet at http://dnb.dnb.de.

© 2023 Walter de Gruyter GmbH, Berlin/Boston
This volume is text- and page-identical with the hardback published in 2022.
Printing and binding: CPI books GmbH, Leck

www.degruyter.com

Acknowledgments

This book derives from several years of research. Along the way I had the privilege and the pleasure to discuss its different layers with many colleagues and friends, a discourse that honed and refined the project. Particular thanks go to Maria Lilla' Montagnani, Maayan Mazor and Ariel Bendor.

I thank the participants of the workshop held at Freie Universität by Susanne Zepp-Zwirner and Klaus Hoffmann-Holland, and the organizers and participants of the seminar at Ask Centre (Art, Science and Knowledge) at Bocconi University. In addition, I would like to thank the participants of the faculty seminars held at the Faculty of Law at the Hebrew University of Jerusalem and at the Faculty of Law at the University of Haifa.

I thank Michal Alberstein and the participants of the seminar on Non-Adversarial Justice (under the auspices of the European Research Council) for their useful comments. Thanks also to Moriel Arev, May Shindler and Noa Sulzer-Achouche for their dedicated and most valuable research assistance.

I wish to thank Ruvik Danieli and Rina Hochman for their careful and dedicated work on the manuscript and for their involvement in bringing it to its final form. Special thanks are due to Shlomit Feldman, who attentively and competently accompanied me alongside the process of preparing the manuscript for publishing.

I am grateful to the Research Authority at the University of Haifa for the support.

Finally, I would like to thank De Gruyter's editors and staff for the meticulous professionalism that was devoted to the production of my work. I would like to thank Daniela Carpi and Klaus Stierstorfer for kindly welcoming this book into their *law and literature* excellent series. Warm thanks to Myrto Aspioti, who has attended the publication process from the very beginning, for her friendly and wise comments and suggestions. Also, I thank Stella Diedrich and Ulla Schmidt for all their help during the advanced stages of the process.

https://doi.org/10.1515/9783110766110-001

Contents

Introduction

It was probably the stories of Greek mythology that ignited my future academic passion: the intersection of law and literature. I grew up in an ancient Mediterranean port city, where the distant past is always palpable. It is a city, mentioned in sources from the Iron Age, on which the Phoenicians, the ancient mariners who cast anchor in many Mediterranean ports, left their mark, and also a city that boasts Hellenistic heritage.[1] It is a city whose wall and moat resonate with centuries of sieges, battles, destruction, ruin, and regeneration. Most notably, it is site that poignantly presents the symbiosis between sea and land. This might have been the sea on which a thousand ships were launched in the chase after Helen of Troy or the waters on which Odysseus may have spent part of his long journey. It is a sea that triggers enchantment with these mythological tales.

Over time, however, I became aware of the discrepancy between the attraction of these mythological stories and the discomfort they aroused. Beneath these tales of heroism and glory lurked discordance that stems from what I now – from a distance of decades, and wearing my scholar's cap – identify as recognition of the unbearable price of lawlessness. While writing this book, the elusive threads linking ancient myths, my own history, and many years of pursuing law and literature gained perceptibility.

This book introduces the Homeric oeuvre into the law and literature canon. In view of the *Iliad* and the *Odyssey*'s unique cultural centrality and the broad canvas created by the law and literature discourse since the 1970s, one might expect to find extensive preoccupation with the Homeric epic and its connection to law and justice. Although other works belonging to the legacy of ancient Greece – especially, of course, Aeschylus' *Oresteia* trilogy and others from the corpus of ancient Greek drama – have become a focus of this discourse, the Homeric epics have remained largely on its margins.[2]

---

1 The city's Hellenistic name was Ptolomaïs. Ptolemy II, who occupied the territories of Syria and Palestine, named this city after his father, Ptolemy I (Barclay Vincent Head, *Historia Numorum: A Manual of Greek Numismatics* (Oxford: Claredon Press, 1911), 788. Ptolemy I founded the Library of Alexandria, and initiated the editing and canonization of the *Iliad* and the *Odyssey*, which had no uniform text at the time (Charles Fredrick Partington, *The British Cyclopedia of Biography: Containing the Lives of Distinguished Men of All Ages and Countries, with Portraits, Residences, Autographs, and Monuments* (London: Wm. S. Orr and Co., Amen Corner, Paternoster Row, 1838), 986).

2 Examples of works that deal with the connections between law and Greek drama include Danielle S. Allen, "Law and Greek Tragedy," in *Cambridge Companion to Greek Law & Culture*, eds. David Cohen and Michael Gagarin (Cambridge: Cambridge University Press, 2005), 374–393;

https://doi.org/10.1515/9783110766110-002

As a modern academic discipline, law and literature is generally regarded to have been inaugurated by the publication of James Boyd White's *The Legal Imagination*.[3] I therefore begin by directing attention to the allusions to the Homeric epics in that seminal composition. It is unsurprising that White turns to these epics when attempting to describe how a story gradually accrues layers of meaning and its circles of influence expand. Imagine, he suggests, that you are telling a story that is not intended to generate any general or theoretical meaning; for instance, a story about a soldier who returns home after many years. The longer the story continues to circulate, the more it becomes possible to identify trends and themes pulling in contrary directions – action versus reflexivity, adventurism versus tranquility and domesticity, life versus death. These are the qualities that found their way into the fabric of the *Odyssey*, which once was a mere collection of stories. The development of the *Iliad* represents a similar process. There once was a poet who decided to tell a tale about the wrath of the hero Achilles, who abandoned the battlefield after being deprived of his spoils of war, and later decided to return. Yet that selfsame poet – or perhaps it was some other – was unable to ignore the brutal nature of the battle and the losses it entailed, the moral significance of Achilles' actions, and the possibility that they expressed not only protest against Agamemnon, but a revolt against the entire heroic enterprise. As White concludes, "to write a story is very often to find that one has written more than one knew,"[4] appositely illustrating his point with the *Odyssey*, which remains to this day one of the most striking examples of a story that gradually accumulated new layers of meaning changing and grown richer, expanding its circles of influence over generations.

Yet, although the Homeric epics already powerfully evoke legal imagination – including the way in which we imagine justice and injustice – and the need to develop a defense for individuals and for the public against raging fury, White skips several centuries forward to the *Oresteia* to demonstrate how a powerful story may be connected to the vast subject of justice: The century begins with Aeschylus' play the *Oresteia*, which tells the story of retaliatory justice in the house of Atreus – a chain of vengeance that continues through generations without end – and celebrates the foundation of a public institution for trial and pun-

---

Maria Aristodemou, *Law & Literature: Journeys from Her to Eternity* (Oxford: Oxford University Press, 200); Edward Monroe Harris, Delfim Ferreira Leao and P. J. Rhodes (eds.), *Law and Drama in Ancient Greece* (London: Bristol Classical Press, Bloomsbury Academic, 2012).
3 See James B. White, *The Legal Imagination: Studies in the Nature of Legal Thought and Expression* (Boston: Little, Brown, 1973) (hereinafter abbreviated as: White 1973).
4 White 1973, 864.

ishment, which is instrumental in allowing the community to bring the narrative of perpetual destruction to a close.

Before expanding on the rationale of this study and its structure, two preliminary remarks are due. The focus here is on an analysis of the *Iliad* and the *Odyssey* as literary texts that contain various representations of law and its absence. The following chapters do not treat the texts from the usual standpoint of classical scholarship and are therefore situated beyond debates between Classics and Ancient History scholars on the Homeric question, the correspondence between history and literature or between myth and reality, and analyses of whether myth does or does not represent religious faith. Nor am I concerned with summarizing developments in Homeric analysis, many of which are already available. The discussion here focuses on the epics as literary works relevant to law. More specifically, the focus of my interest is the status of the works as literary texts, particularly as works that narrate myths that have cultivated notions pertaining to the naissance of law.

"It goes against my grain to repeat a tale told once, and told so clearly,"[5] says Odysseus to his Phaeacian audience (*Odyssey* 12.490 – 491), juxtaposing humility and arrogance. But these words perhaps even better illustrate the power ingrained in the repetition of stories already told. The myths about the Trojan War, the wrath of Achilles, Hector's death, and Odysseus' prolonged return to Ithaca had passed from generation to generation even before Homer recorded them. Their very survival attests to their reception by previous generations. Homer retells them in his own way, and apparently does it best, as according to Moses Finley, Homer "[o]ccupies the first stage in the history of Greek control over its myths."[6] The new story that Homer tells brings to light a fundamental understanding of law and justice. This study highlights and uses these new insights to identify points of correspondence between the transition from myth to tragedy and the gradual transition from a social existence lacking formal law to an institutionalized legal system such as that practiced in the polis.

Through an exploration of the transcendent games that past and future play in literature, it is my aim to contribute to our understanding of the tapestry of stories about the evolution of law. Broadly, this book presents several observations on laws' evolution. First, I aim to show that the Homeric epics represent

---

5 Homer, *The Odyssey*, trans. Robert Fagles (London: The Folio Society, 2001) (hereinafter abbreviated as: *Odyssey*). The story of the Greek victory in the Trojan War, from which Odysseus returns, is told in Homer, *The Iliad of Homer*, trans. Robert Fagles (London: The Folio Society, 2001) (hereinafter abbreviated as: *Iliad*).

6 Moses I. Finley, *The World of Odysseus* (Harmondsworth: Penguin, 1972), 29 (hereinafter abbreviated as: Finley 1972).

a significant milestone in the long conceptualization of Greek law. Second, I suggest that the Homeric epics prefigure, perhaps even necessarily so, the main story of the regimentation and juridification of anger that later appears in the *Oresteia*. Finally, from the perspective of female agency, I argue that the newly institutionalized law represented in the *Oresteia* blocks paths of action that had been available to women in the Homeric epics.

A second remark concerns the use of the term "law." The law does not exist a priori. It is not a material field whose establishment and stages of development are amenable to capture, tracking, and rigorous description. The law is an abstract concept, a complex and multifaceted intellectual continuum. The development of the system of law and the legal institutions that operated in Athens was influenced by multiple factors, including emerging social needs and power struggles between groups and interests. Other factors included norms and practices concerning the resolution of the tension between individual interests and the public interest, insights that developed and gradually seeped into collective consciousness through various means, including through powerful narratives. Within such an evolutionary conception of the law, an important contribution is made by an analysis of the stories that gradually structured the law and of the overt and covert intersections between the legal field and other fields.

The first chapter lays the theoretical foundation for the reading of the epics this book puts forward, beginning with an elaboration of the concept of generative legal narratives. Generative legal narratives, stories about the shift from a lawless society to a society that embraces the rule of law, shape the way we imagine law, establish our expectations of the law, and design potential ways of changing or reforming law. As mentioned earlier, the *Oresteia* is one of the major generative legal narratives in western cultural reserves. The following chapters discuss how the emergence of this work was facilitated by notions that were prefigured several centuries earlier in the Homeric epics.

The first chapter begins with the literature alongside law paradigm, which suggests several possible prisms of inquiry into the nature of the links between the two fields. One such prism focuses on narratives dealing with the absence of law and the consequences of such absence for the human condition. Another prism of inquiry points to a careful scrutiny of law's failures and limits: "Always mistrust the law," as the ancient maxim goes.[7] No matter which prism is selected, the literature alongside law paradigm critically examines the conceptualiza-

---

7 This maxim, reported by Nicole Castan, is quoted in David Cohen, *Law, Violence, and Community in Classical Athens* (Cambridge, UK; New York: Cambridge University Press, 1995), 23 (hereinafter abbreviated as: Cohen 1995).

tion of law as an autonomous, self-contained system. Literature makes us realize how incomplete the law is when it stands alone: Law realizes its full potential only when set within a broader context. As David Cohen maintains, it would be naïve to assume that legal institutions emerge to meet "societal needs" or result from the beneficial operation of some invisible hand. The *law* and legal norms that existed in fifth-century BC Athens "should not be judged according to a set of independent norms, but rather as a part of ongoing process that began long before the particular trial and will [...] continue into the future."[8] Such a trajectory is emblematic of intellectual and moral evolution, but also of "competitive efforts of groups and individuals to pursue their enmities, advance their interests, and to recall the traditional Greek definition of justice, to help their friends and harm their enemies" (*The Republic*, 332d–335c).[9] A re-analysis, then, of the Homeric epics, equipped with the law alongside literature perspective, should reveal significant landmarks on the long path of progress of law in general, and of Greek law in particular.

The second chapter opens with an exposition of the similarity between situations that could be considered a crisis of revenge that stand at the center of both the *Odyssey* and the *Oresteia*. The Oresteia deals with a warrior-king who returns victorious but is murdered by his wife and her lover upon his return. Orestes, his son, exacts revenge by murdering his mother, triggering the fury of the Erinyes, goddesses of revenge. To end the conflict and the cycle of vengeance, Athena establishes a court. Orestes is brought to trial, and acquitted. The *Odyssey*, too, deals with a warrior-king who returns home victorious. He, however, encounters a band of audacious suitors who have pestered his faithful wife for years and consumed his property. He takes revenge by murdering them. The *Odyssey*, however, makes no mention of a judicial resolution or of the murderer's accountability for his actions. As a result, it will not be the cunning trickster Odysseus who lights the eternal fire of the torch of law, but rather by tormented, anguished Orestes.

This chapter illuminates the poetic, performative, and sociopolitical considerations in the *Odyssey* that prepared the ground for the emergence of a generative legal narrative in the *Oresteia*, and suggests that the *Odyssey* constitutes a significant milestone on the path to the generative legal narrative. Epic poetry generally, and the *Odyssey* in particular, sketches a sophisticated social milieu in which economics, politics, warfare, and social and family life are conducted in accordance with known norms and rules. Its heroes are responsive to social

---

8 Cohen 1995, 23.
9 Cohen 1995, 23.

authority, and they exhibit some degree of subservience to the social order and its values. The Homeric communities function through a discourse that takes place in the public sphere, at assemblies. These assemblies are instrumental in regulating the interactions between community members and leaders, allowing social life to be conducted. Even in the absence of written laws, the assemblies furnish a certain representation of the principle of deliberation and practices that we would now ascribe to the field of public law. Furthermore, the world of the epics is not entirely unfamiliar with judicial or quasi-judicial procedure, and its protagonists follow rules that define the course of revenge recounted in the *Iliad*. The epics, then, already reflect contemplations on reckoning, retribution, justice, and public order.

And yet, the pre-generative story told by the *Odyssey* conveys a picture of law afflicted by inherent failures, since the model it presents primarily serves the interests of the privileged patriarchal elite. As much as the *Odyssey* recounts the exploits of an elite that pays a relatively small price for its offenses, not much will change in a formal rule of law according to the *Oresteia*. Orestes, who is a member of this elite, is ultimately exempted from legal restitution for the murder he committed. The elite will continue to enjoy privileges.

Finally, the discussion sheds light on the figure of Athena as a symbol of both the expectations and hopes conserning the law, and its failures. Already in the *Odyssey*, Athena represents the potential of judicial process as encompassing a wide range of possibilities, including the flexibility to deviate from the formal judicial model in favor of a rhetorical-persuasive model that expands the available means of conflict resolution. In the *Odyssey*, Athena is a quasi-mediator who aspires to craft a peace pact that is beneficial to society at large. In the *Oresteia*, Athena becomes an adversarial judge who administers the court according to formal rules. In both cases, Athena comes across as a judge acting in accordance with the zeitgeist, but also as a deeply flawed judge whose partiality in favor of the masculine over the feminine is brazenly self-declared. In both cases the law comes across as an instrument of conflict resolution and peace, but also as one that is malformed.

In the third chapter, the discussion delves into the connection between the Homeric epics and law by turning the spotlight on the destructive consequences of unbridled wrath. Anger is a key concept that has always been linked to law. In effect, the ability and authority to regiment anger lies at the root of most legal systems. The subjugation of the impulse to act out of anger to procedures dictated by the law is a core fundament of the rule of law. The Homeric epics represent an appropriate and perhaps even prerequisite prequel to the central story of regimentation and juridification of anger that assumes a more structured form in the *Oresteia*. The third chapter contrasts the wrath of the two major epic heroes,

Achilles and Odysseus. The *Iliad*'s narrative posits Achilles' wrath as a central topic already in its first line, and it subsequently becomes clear that he is serially enraged. The *Iliad* describes three successive waves of fury that sow increasingly devastating consequences. Odysseus' wrath, by contrast, is not framed as a central element of the narrative, and is not a theme on which Homer elaborates. Still, a close look at Odysseus' wrath, which comes to a crescendo in a spectacle of fury, costs the lives of Ithaca's nobility and the dozen serving women of Odysseus' household.

The question that the epics explore is whether the terrible costs to society exacted by the eruption of fury are unavoidable. Tragedy, presided by Aeschylus' Athena, offers an answer that stems from the new understandings and new values represented by the polis, first and foremost the need to devise defenses against murderous rage in the interests of society as a whole. The law is the tool by means of which these defenses will be implemented. As an institution that belongs to society at large, the law highlights the divergence between the private interest of the mythical hero and the collective interest of society. Achilles and Odysseus bore no responsibility for the many deaths they caused, and in cultural consciousness they ended their days as heroes haloed in glory. The tragic hero Orestes, however, was subject to a new conception that drew a link between action and accountability. He would be judged by the new institution established by Athena atop the Areopagus, and would ultimately be saved by a tie from suffering harm for his actions. Thus, the generative narrative of the evolution of law is distilled out of the epics that centered upon the malignant outcomes of unbridled wrath. Unfortunately, as the generative story itself demonstrates, and as the future reiterates, the law would not prove to be an efficient or reliant mechanism for justly resolving conflicts or for achieving truth and justice. It would gradually become clear that the law is part of an ongoing human endeavor, studded with good and bad intentions, with the power to protect the social order as well as the capacity to serve whoever would disrupt it.

The fourth chapter proposes to reconceptualize the *Odyssey* as a unique moment on the continuum of the conflict between the sexes. In effect, the *Odyssey* is female driven: The *Odyssey* tells of queens, princesses, goddesses, and serving women who manage to determine courses of events. The pre-judicial era of the epics grant women some freedom of action, as long as it is discreetly exercised or disguised. The social system strikes a balance between male dominance and feminine agency: In this social and political environment focused on male will and interest, women are allowed some degree of freedom to promote their own interests, choices and desires by operating outside the default androcentric options of action. Homeric society represents what I denote the *Metis Syndrome*. It is a spectrum of behaviors that represent women's power alongside the need to conceal its manifestations from the public eye. The *Metis Syndrome* clarifies some puzzling aspects of the enigmatic figure of Penelope, and adds depth to the figures of Calypso, Circe, Arete, Nausicaa, and the serving women whose voices also can be heard in the epic. Chapter four adds another layer to the analysis of the Homeric figure of Athena, arguing that in significant ways she is closer to ideals of justice and equality than the Athena of tragedy.

On the stage of history, the *Metis Syndrome* eventually dissipates. Future society, which gives birth to the rule of law, also blocks the restricted spectrum of female agency reflected in the Homeric epics. The era of tragedy decides unequivocally in favor of male superiority, to the constant service of which the newly minted rule of law would be harnessed and committed.

Chapter 1
Law and Story

Odysseus paused... They all fell silent,
hushed, his story holding them spellbound... (Odyssey 11.368–369)

Introduction

The *polis*-world that existed in the fifth century BC came to be labeled as a culture that established legal institutions and promoted the universal importance and power of written laws.[10] This legal turn was not a miraculous event, and was not the result of some invisible hand. The numerous factors that facilitated its emergence include the invention of writing and "the recognition of public space as the center of the community and the establishment of a minimum authority vested in the community."[11] Intellectual and moral evolution, together with growing social tensions and a need for greater internal stability, also contributed to the process.[12] The connective tissue required to mobilize all these factors toward the creation of a new legal regime was supplied by a generative legal narrative – an account of the transition from lawless existence to a society that adopts the rule of law; a story sufficiently potent to incorporate politics, elite interests, and new societal demands into the notion of the rule of law.

In the *Odyssey*, stories related by bards constitute communications in the public sphere. Odysseus, a master storyteller himself, describes the shared public experience:

> There is nothing better
> Than when deep joy holds way throughout the realm
> And banqueters up down the palace sit in ranks,
> Enthralled to hear the bard [...] (*Odyssey 9.5–8*)

The stories told by the bards continued to evolve in the following generations into stories told that were eventually reworked by Greek play writers. The generative legal narrative in the *Oresteia* is a most prominent example of a highly in-

---

10 Karl J. Holkeskamp, "Arbitrators, Lawgivers and the 'Codification of Law' in Archaic Greece: Problems and Perspectives," *Metis. Anthropologie des mondes anciens* 7 (1992): 51 (hereinafter abbreviated as Holkeskamp 1992).

11 Holkeskamp 1992, 64.

12 Holkeskamp 1992, 67.

https://doi.org/10.1515/9783110766110-003

strumental narrative in its own right, whose emergence was facilitated by a process that included the telling and retelling of the ideas in the Homeric narratives, which preceded the *Oresteia* by several centuries.

This chapter commences with a review of the links between law and story, and the concept of generative legal narratives, and then introduces the *law alongside literature* paradigm that offers a theoretical framework for addressing the interrelationships between law and literature. The discussion of this paradigm proceeds as follows: First, adopting the lens of literature to critically examine the inherently limited nature of law and its failures and flaws. Next, establishing the aspiration, triggered by imagination, to modify and improve the law. Equipped with the *law alongside literature* perspective, we return to the Homeric epics to reveal significant landmarks on the long trail of the evolution of law in general and of Greek law in particular. Finally addressing the significance, particularly now in this digital age more than ever, of maintaining a vibrant appreciation of the generative legal narratives of ancient stories that remind us how essential legal constructs and institutions came into existence.

"Law begins … after narrative"

Our social existence is organized around narratives.[13] One can attribute a significant part of human experience to the immense repository of narratives that produce meaning and organize different realms of reality.[14] As Jonathan Culler aptly put it:

> Stories, the argument goes, are the main way we make sense of things, whether in thinking of our lives as progression leading somewhere or in telling ourselves what is happening in the world. […] It [life] follows not a scientific logic of cause and effect but the logic of a story, where to understand is to conceive how one thing leads to another, how something might have come about […].[15]

---

13 The definition of narrative, its substance, functioning and the relationship between it and the plot, are issues that have attracted extensive research. See e.g., Peter Brooks, *Reading for the Plot: Design and Intention in Narrative* (New York: A.A. Knopf, 1984) (hereinafter abbreviated as Brooks 1984); Jonathan Culler, *Literary Theory: A Very Short Introduction* (Oxford; New York: Oxford University Press, 1997), 83–94 (hereinafter abbreviated as Culler 1997); Shlomit Rimmon-Kenan, *Narrative Fiction: Contemporary Poetics* (London: Routledge, 2003).
14 Regarding the centrality of narrative in human experience see Brooks 1984; Culler 1997, 83–94; Michael Roemer, *Telling Stories: Postmodernism and the Invalidation of Traditional Narrative* (Lanham, MD: Rowman & Littlefield, 1995).
15 Culler 1997, 83–84.

Narrative organizes information in a way that constitutes a special mode of knowing. Since certain stories are etched into memory, and the exposure of many people to the same stories creates a collective consciousness and shared cultural capital that enable communal understandings. In such stories lies the basis for shared human perceptions and beliefs, agreements, and activities, and the foundation for change, growth, and development.

Narrative's key role in creating concepts of self and society has become clear in various fields, including those addressing law-related issues, such as race, community, gender, and the practice of law.[16] Indeed, "Law begins ... *after* narrative."[17]

A significant contribution to the study of the links between law and narrative can be attributed to the discipline of law and literature. A critical element of legal practice is mastery of "both sorts of discourse (both narrative and analysis) and put[ting] them to work, at the same time and despite their inconsistencies, in the service of a larger enterprise."[18] Since narrative permeates the domain of law and operates within it on multiple levels, in previous works I delineated a map of legal narratives and proposed a typology of the law's dependencies on narrative, reflecting the ways in which law and narrative continuously intertwine.[19] Here I focus on the first of the three prominent forms of legal narratives – generative narratives, conceptualizing narratives, and functional narratives.[20]

Generative Legal Narratives

Glanville Williams referred to law as "a collection of symbols capable of evoking ideas and emotions, together with the ideas and emotions so evoked."[21] What, however, is the force that unites certain expressions and transforms them into "symbols" that represent "law"? Can we locate, define, or even imagine this transformative event, the moment when law emerged? Jacques Derrida famously

---

16 David M. Engel, "Origin Myths: Narratives of Authority, Resistance, Disability, and Law," *Law & Society Review* 27.4 (1993): 785–826, 789–790.

17 Anthony G. Amsterdam and Jerome S. Bruner, *Minding the Law* (Cambridge, MA: Harvard University Press, 2000), 283 (hereinafter abbreviated as: Amsterdam and Bruner 2000).

18 Amsterdam and Bruner 2000, 283.

19 See Shulamit Almog, "Windows and 'Windows': Reflections on Law and Literature in the Digital Age," *University of Toronto Law Journal* 57.4 (2007): 755–780 (hereinafter abbreviated as Almog 2007).

20 For elaboration on conceptualizing legal narratives and functional legal narratives, see Almog 2007, 90–102.

21 Glanville Williams, "Language and the Law," *Law Quarterly Review* 61 (1945): 71–86, 86.

expressed a version of this query: "How are we to distinguish between the force of law of a legitimate power and the supposedly original violence that must have established this authority?"[22] Derrida emphasizes the violence that characterized the moment of law's emergence, and he is probably correct, but violence alone cannot suffice. The transformation is contingent on a type of enchantment that is sometimes generated by words, by the evocative power of a story that holds its audience spellbound. This power of enchantment is an essential feature of generative legal narratives.

Generative legal narratives perform three functions. First, they are the stories that negotiate the transition from lawless existence to a social existence under the rule of law. They shape the way we imagine law, they establish our expectations of the law, and outline potential ways of changing or reforming law. Second, law requires such narratives in order to maintain a constant acknowledgment of its legitimacy and authority and to address oppositions of all kinds. Every legal regime draws legitimacy and authority from some generative narrative. As Robert Cover states,

> For every constitution there is an epic, for each Decalogue a scripture [...] law and narrative are inseparably related. Every prescription is insistent in its demand to be located in discourse – to be supplied with history and destiny, beginning and end, explanation and purpose.[23]

Generative narratives are continually activated in our consciousness even if no direct reference is made to them during the daily function of law's machinery. They continue to accrue symbols, knowledge, and other stories – both new and recurring – that are associated with the idea of law. Generative narratives contain a unique element of dynamism that remains ever-operative in the collective mind.

Finally, law relies on narrative to make sense of basic, organizing legal ideas. Thus, for example, we employ organizing narratives to conceptualize notions of liability and responsibility. As Guyora Binder and Robert Weisberg explain, "an assignment of casual responsibility involves a short *chain* of casual explanation, a simple narrative linking a harmful result to a blameworthy character."[24] Similarly, there is a narrative of property (this is mine, so I can do *whatever* I

---

22 Jacques Derrida, "Force of Law: The 'Mystical Foundation of Authority' (Deconstruction and the Possibility of Justice)," *Cardozo Law Review* 11.5–6 (1990): 920–1045, 927.

23 Robert M. Cover, *Narrative, Violence, and the Law: The Essays of Robert Cover*, eds. Martha Minow, Michael Ryan, and Austin Sarat (Ann Arbor: University of Michigan Press, 1992), 96.

24 Guyora Binder and Robert Weisberg, *Literary Criticisms of Law* (Princeton, NJ: Princeton University Press, 2000), 264.

want with it), a narrative of contracts (I reached an agreement with you, and agreements must be honored), a narrative of constitutional law (we need to define and protect superior norms to maintain social order), and so on.

However, generative narratives often contain a subversive seed, and enfold not only the potential to entrench the existing social order, but also to challenge it. The slavery story, for example, can be interpreted as a story that strengthens law by demonstrating law's self-rectifying potential. Yet the same story may function as a constant reminder of law's failure to address injustice. Such opposed understandings illuminate the unique properties of the narrative mode of knowing, and specifically its potential to concurrently validate and challenge our cultural practices.

There are many modes of generative narratives. Some of them might be referred to as secondary generative narratives, which shape and define legal categories, concepts, and principles. They are created, for example, by historical occurrences. Thus, the constitutional narratives of the United States of America include stories about the colonies' quest for religious freedom and stories of slavery during the civil war. The principles of American constitutional law are drawn from those stories.

Similar qualities characterize generative narratives that originate from other cultural sources, such as scripture, canonical works of philosophy, psychology or political thought, and significant historical events. Milner S. Ball, for example, illustrates the important role of biblical stories in our perceptions of legal practices.[25] Thus, the story of Moses receiving the law at Mount Sinai, and the way in which Moses represents both God and the Hebrew people at the same time, produces a major narrative of legal advocacy that is associated with the practice of modern lawyers.[26] In Ball's reading, the story of Rachel, weeping for her children, "transcends both law and morality"[27] and God's response creates a fundamental narrative relevant both to law's capacity to accommodate things too deep for words,"[28] and to contemporaneous legal issues such as the role of emotion in the judicial process. As Ball emphasizes, though the biblical narratives' initial audiences were the first communities of Jews and Christians, those narratives were never limited to religious communities, nor were they designed to be.

---

25 Milner S. Ball, *Called by Stories: Biblical Sagas and Their Challenge for Law* (Durham, NC: Duke University Press, 2000), 4 (hereinafter abbreviated as Ball 2000).

26 Ball 2000, 9–21.

27 Ball 2000, 89.

28 Ball 2000, 1.

Their "fundamental and freeing"[29] qualities have been available to all audiences, at all times since, and to present-day legal discourse.

The *Oresteia*, which comprises three plays – *Agamemnon*, *Choēphoroe*, and *Eumenidēs* – tells the story of Agamemnon's son Orestes, who kills his mother and her lover to revenge his father's murder. Orestes is pursued by the Furies, the avenging goddesses, and flees from Argos to Delphi and then to Athens. The goddess Athena proposes to settle the dispute by holding a tribunal on the Areopagus, establishing the first court of justice. Orestes is acquitted and is allowed to return to Argos. Athena thus ends the vicious perpetual circle of violence, and founds a new order, the rule of law.

The constitutive moment of the judicial procedure described in the *Eumenides* is central to the conceptualization of the rule of law, and deserves to be classified as a generative legal narrative. However, a generative legal narrative can emerge only at a certain moment in history, against the background of preceding narratives that chartered its course, in some sense. The evolutionary path of the rule of law established by Athena in the *Oresteia* can be traced to an earlier past, one in which the *Odyssey*, with its powerful reflection on reckoning, retribution, justice and public order, constitutes a major milestone. In the *Oresteia*, these reflections have evolved into a generative legal narrative. It is this path, which associates the Homeric epics with the generative legal narrative represented in Aeschylus' *Oresteia*,[30] that this book reconstructs.

The *Law alongside Literature* Paradigm

A still common practice is the subdivision of the law and literature discourse into two principle fields: "law as literature" and "law in literature."[31] The study of law as literature seeks to apply the methods and terminology used in literary criti-

---

29 Ball 2000, 6.

30 The Oresteia trilogy by Aeschylus: *Agamemnon*; *The Eumenides*; *The Libation Bearers*. All translations by Hugh Lloyd-Jones, 1970.

31 Simon Stern, "Literary Analysis of Law," in *The Oxford Handbook of Legal History*, eds. Markus D. Dubber and Christopher L. Tomlins (Oxford: Oxford University Press, 2018), 63–78. Stern yet notes that "over the last ten or fifteen years, this conventional formula has become increasingly untenable, as scholars have explored a much wider array of questions relating to literary and literary forms, concepts, methods, dispositions, and media" (2). The *law alongside literature* paradigm presented here pertains indeed to the vogue of dispensing with the coupling of "law in literature" and "law as literature," and exploring, instead, how legal and literary constructs can be simultaneously explored.

cism to the internal needs of law, such as the analysis of legal texts or the evaluation of legal poetics and rhetoric. The main concern of law in literature is the contribution made by literary works to the better understanding of law and legal mechanisms. Thus, both sub-disciplines share the position that literature is to be studied primarily in service of law, whether by enhancing our understanding of how law operates, disclosing law's limitations and flaws, or using literary accounts to support normative statements – implicit or explicit – about the law.

There is, however, another way to view the relationship between the two disciplines: as a paradigm unfettered by the hierarchical implications of conventional categorizations. I call this *"law alongside literature."*[32] This paradigm reveals the elasticity of the boundaries separating law and literature, and the fluidity that characterizes their interactions. It emphasizes the indispensable links between distinctive cultural systems and the impossibility of creating permanent boundaries or impermeable enclaves of discourse. The *law alongside literature* paradigm depicts both law and literature as social practices in constant interaction. It contends that aesthetics and poetics are an inextricable part of law, just as legal and ethical structures are an essential part of aesthetic expression, and illuminates, for example, that generative legal narratives continuously serve as one of the formative as well as change-inducing forces of legal activity.

The *law alongside literature* paradigm involves two stages of inquiry. The first critically examines the conception of law as a holistic, autonomous, self-contained system by emphasizing the inherently flawed nature of law. Both the *Iliad* and the *Odyssey* reflect such processes. Both depict lawless societies of men and women killing and being killed, subjected to uncontrolled ferocity and brutal deaths. Both epics also allude to tentative notions of remedy. From the narrative focus on the unbearable toll of unharnessed brutality, wrath, and force emerges the viable option of building societal defenses.

Already in the *Iliad*, in the famous description of Achilles' shield,[33] these two options are embedded in the description of the two cities. One is a safe, happy city, where residents celebrate weddings and feasts and congregate in the market place, and where disputes are resolved in a communal space and determined by "the judge who'd speak the straightest verdict" (*Iliad* 18.592). In the second city, strife, havoc, and violent death pervade society:

> now seizing a man alive with fresh wounds [...]
> Now howling a dead man through the slaughter by the heels (*Iliad* 18.624–625).

---

32 E.g., Shulamit Almog, "Literature alongside law as a contemporary paradigm," *Cultural Dynamics* 13.1 (2001): 53–65; Almog 2007.
33 *Iliad*, Book XVIII.

The overwhelming, inexplicable brutality is juxtaposed with a peaceful, governed social existence. The fate of the city of Troy resonates this duality.

Both the *Odyssey* and the *Oresteia* augment the meaning of the *law alongside literature* paradigm. Both are meaningful stations on law's long avolution. The *Iliad* ends with the burial of Hector, which is overshadowed by fear of further attacks and utter destruction of the once thriving and peaceful city. The *Odyssey* concludes with a reference to measures that should be taken by society in order to prevent such dire fate: "And Athena handed down her pacts of peace between both sides for all the years to come". (*Odyssey* 24.599–600). Agreement promotes peace and prevents further violence. As the origin story of the legal system and legal institutions, the Homeric epics introduce the need for law by highlighting the individual and societal price incurred by its absence. This spore will ultimately evolve into the generative legal narrative presented in *the Oresteia*.

The second stage of an inquiry guided by the *law alongside literature* paradigm focuses on negotiating the limits and failures of law. Literature reveals law's faults, but it does not negate the notion of law altogether. Like law, literature manifests the aspiration to achieve a fuller understanding of human existence, although this goal is undermined by the inherent challenges of the human condition. Identifying the limits of law is important for prescribing remedies. Once the failures and flaws of existing law have been identified, the next step is to put things right, to achieve a complex, dynamic equilibrium between law, human needs, and human limitations. Of crucial importance to this task is the literary use of imagination, which can bridge the gap between the needs and interests of the individual and those of the community. Imagination does this by cultivating the faculty of empathy, that is, by developing sensitivity for the suffering of others as well as the capacity to identify with them. Through the process of empathetic imagination, the other is transformed into one of us, deepening our acknowledgment of their pain. The facilitation of this process, which leads to human solidarity, is one of the main assets of literature. If the first stage of the *law alongside literature* paradigm inquiry clarifies the conflict between individual and public and stresses the difficulties the law faces in dealing with it, the second stage of inquiry uses narratives that derive from imagination to suggest possible solutions. Narratives focusing upon the plight of individuals enhance sensitivity and attentiveness to others. Imagination embedded in literary narratives supports law's effort to satisfy the human needs of all subjects of a legal order.

This duality is embedded in the generative narrative pertaining to the establisher of criminal justice in *Oresteia*. Athena emphasizes that the new social instrument that she is establishing – the rule of law – is primarily designed to serve male interests: "For there is no mother who gave birth to me and I approve the male principle in all things and with all my heart" (*Eumenides* 736–738). Patriarchal domination of women becomes a constituting principle of the new legal system. Orestes' acquittal is based upon the fact that he killed a woman, and not a man. Literature depicts law from its inception as a tool serving men and wronging women.

Yet the story Aeschylus recounts in the *Oresteia* is not a story of the triumph of justice, equity, or dignity. It is primarily a story about achieving social stability, and, more specifically, it is the formative story of this new tool, the rule of law, and its instrumental role in perpetuating the dominance of upper-class men.

As the paradigm of *law alongside literature* proclaims, law is a tremendous accomplishment. It reflects the most sophisticated aspects of human social existence. The law is also prone to mistakes and failures, yet these can be addressed; it is capable of protecting and perpetuating social order, but can be instrumental in its destruction. History after the *Oresteia* will reveal that law is a constantly evolving mechanism. The continuous flow of *law alongside literature* supports the unremitting hope of bettering the law.

Reading Homer in Digital Age

"This week I hosted a reception for the friends of our university," said the Rector in her welcome speech. "One of our most generous friends, a wonderful guy [...] asked me, 'Tell me, Liora, why do you need to teach Humanities in your university?' [...] "I told him, 'Amnon, tell me – what is the most important feature of a high-tech entrepreneur?'" He instantly answered: 'Imagination, creativity, originality.'... "Very nice," I told him. "These are precisely the qualities advanced by the humanities. It is well known that the most famous names in the Silicon Valley do not send their kids to study programming, but to knit and to read the Iliad and the Odyssey."[34]

The opening quote, taken from a 2021 novel by Maya Arad, is a satiric vignette describing the rector of a prominent university doing her best to convince her audience that scholarship in the humanities, and in particular reading Homer's epics, is beneficial if one aims to excel in the STEM disciplines (science, technology, engineering, and mathematics). Amusing as they these lines are, they capture important contemporary debates on the relevance of studying the archaic methods of storytelling in the digital age. Are technological advances threatening to erode the power of generative narratives, or can we continue to look to these narratives as a source of insights pertinent to contemporary law?

---

34 Maya Arad, *All about Abigail*. Ben Shemen: Modan / Xargol Books. (Hebrew), 244 (Hebrew, my translation).

From its emergence, digital technology was recognized for its potential to change the systems by which meaning is traditionally produced and received. That potential is being realized with increasing momentum, creating what might be called a "digital condition." The term "condition" conveys the sense that digital possibilities not only create revolutionary technological options that affect culture at large, but because of their encompassing nature, also create a new experience, state of being, and state of mind. Digital technology permeates epistemology in a manner that renders the digital condition inseparable from the construction of meaning.

In the digital age, most of the stories to which we are exposed are digitally produced, visually loaded and clipped, disseminated, and rapidly consumed. Legal fields have not remained impervious to the infiltration of new cultural habits, such as shorter attention spans and the continuous consumption of instant, rapidly changing audio-visual messages.[35] The incessant digital outpouring of fragmented images may lead to poetic failure, undermining the capacity to create and receive structured stories that demand time, attentiveness, and narrative awareness. One potential outcomes of this inundation of digital messages is the law's diminishing capacity to benefit from literary narratives that previously supported and sustained its practices. Literature constitutes an extensive collective reservoir that always stands at our disposal as a body of knowledge, as a vital source of meaningful images, and as a stimulus that ignites the imagination and generates changes, yet the constant deluge of digital images, sounds, sights, and experiences might undermine our ability to focus on structured, lengthy epics.

It is not yet clear how narrative cognizance will adapt to the digital condition. New modes of storytelling and story listening are rapidly evolving along with hybrid forms of poetics, and can be expected to transform the stories that serve as legal representations. Narratives in courts may become much shorter, faster, clip-oriented, heavily augmented with visual images, and subjected to sophisticated audio and visual editing. Some of these novel methods of representation are already in place in the legal domain. It is early to tell how will law look, read, and sound and how literature will fare in a technology saturated environment. Law is very much in need of literature to maintain a sense of clear

---

35 In another work I elaborated on this issue, and while distinguishing between different types of narratives that function in the legal realm, explained how they are influenced by the digital condition. See Shulamit Almog, "From Sterne and Borges to Lost Storytellers: Cyberspace, Narrative, and Law," *Fordham Intellectual Property, Media & Entertainment Law Journal* 13.1 (2002): 1–34 (hereinafter abbreviated as: Almog 2002); Shulamit Almog, "Creating Representations of Justice in the Third Millennium: Legal Poetics in Digital Times," *Rutgers Computer & Technology Law Journal* 32.2. (2006): 183–245.

mission and purpose and to preserve its legitimacy, distinctiveness, and authority. Law is also dependent on perceptions of the self and of others, which have been traditionally produced and maintained by literature, yet literature itself is rapidly evolving, together with novel scholarly developments that offer theories, methods and tools for exploring literature in the digital age.[36]

Alexander Pushkin in his 1827 poem Arion, tells about the ancient Greek legend of Arion, a Greek poet who lived in Corinth. While sailing home after winning a poetry competition in Sicily, he was attacked by his fellow sailors, who attempted to kill him in order to take possession of the prizes he had won. Arion managed to persuade his assailants to let him sing a last song. After singing praise to Apollo, Arion threw himself into the sea, but a dolphin that was attracted by the song saved his life and carried him to land.[37]

Pushkin's borrowed (and altered) use of the ancient Greek legend resonates the dynamism of an evolving literary capital, its capacity to carry us through storms, its capacity to aid in overcoming the upheavals created by unforeseen shifts. It is the bard who survives the storm, and it is the skill of the bard, as Homer tells us, that "serves the house" (*Odyssey* 17.421).

...When suddenly,
A storm! And the wide sea was rearing ...
The helmsman and the crew were lost.
No sailor by the storm was tossed
Ashore – but I, who had been singing.
I chant the songs I loved of yore,
And on the sunned and rocky shore
I dry my robes, all wet and clinging.[38]

---

36 Especially interesting in this context is the highly developing field of digital humanities. For an in-depth analysis of digital humanities see David M. Berry and Anders Fagerjord, *Digital Humanities: Knowledge and Critique in a Digital Age* (Cambridge, UK; Malden, MA: Polity, 2017). Worth noting in this context is *The Homer Multitext Project*, edited by Casey Dué and Mary Ebbott, which "*offers free access to a library of texts and images and tools to allow readers to discover and engage with the Homeric tradition*" (http://www.homermultitext.org/about/).
37 Herodotus, *The Histories*, trans. Robin Waterfield (Oxford, UK: Oxford University Press, 1998), 1.23–24. According to this version of the story, the King of Corinth did not believe Arion's story. The truth was revealed only after the sailors appeared in Corinth, claiming that Arion had decided to remain in Italy, whereupon the traitorous sailors were punished.
38 Alexander Sergeevich Pushkin, *The Poems, Prose, and Plays of Alexander Pushkin*, trans. Avrahm Yarmilinsky (New York: The Modern Library, 1943).

Chapter 2
Law in the *Odyssey* – the Story of Motion

The Odyssey is the story of motion, purposeful and purposeless, successful and futile.
What else is the history of law?
Bernard Schlink, The Reader

Tragedy is born when myth starts to be considered from a point of view of a citizen.
Jean-Pierre Vernant, Myth and Tragedy

Two Ancient Stories

An ancient story tells of a warrior-king who returns home victorious after a long war and arduous journey. He is greeted by a faithful wife and a devoted son, but encounters a group of would-be usurpers. In the years he had struggled to return home, they had harassed the queen and made free with his property. Upon his return, the king kills them all, together with the maidservants suspected of disloyalty. This bloodshed brings peace to the kingdom.

Another ancient story tells of a second king who returns directly home as a victor after the same long and bloody war, approximately a decade before the king of the previous story. Immediately upon his return, he is murdered by his wife and her lover. The king's son avenges his father's murder, killing both his mother and her lover. The Furies, the goddesses of vengeance, seek to exercise their right and duty to avenge the queen's life by taking the life of her son, the murderer. At this point, for the first time in Western history, a court is established: The son/murderer is placed on trial and acquitted. The legal procedure not only breaks the cycle of vengeance but replaces it with a new institution that brings peace to the kingdom.

The first story is told in the *Odyssey*, the celebrated epic poem attributed to Homer, written circa 750–700 BC,[39] which recounts the adventures of King Odysseus of Ithaca, on his return from Troy to his homeland, where he was forced to wrest back control of his kingdom. The second story is related in the *Oresteia*, a trilogy written and staged by Aeschylus in 458 BC consisting

---

Note: A substantially revised version of this chapter was published as "From the Odyssey Onwards: Law's Long and Winding Road" in *Law & Literature* 32.1 (Spring 2020).

39 Finley 1972, 18.

https://doi.org/10.1515/9783110766110-004

of three plays, and considered the greatest achievement of Greek drama.[40, 41] The *Oresteia* tells of the events that leading up to the establishment of the first court in the ancient world, a court that acquitted Orestes, who killed his mother.

Many generations after it was written, the *Oresteia* retains its seminal standing as a generative legal narrative that appears as the backdrop to the law, describing the transition from a lawless existence to the rule of law.[42] The *Odyssey*'s connection to the establishment of law is, however, not usually recognized, and is markedly understated within the law and literature discourse.

As Martin Ostwald describes, literary, archaeological, and epigraphic sources are key among the limited available evidence of the many links in the complex evolution of the law.[43] Indeed, alongside the legal channel flows the literary stream, each enriching the other, influencing and being influenced. The reading proposed here positions the *Odyssey* within the law and literature canon as a significant milestone in the evolution of the law, which led to the generative legal narrative presented in *the Oresteia*.

From Mythic Revenge to Judicial Resolution in Tragedy

The *Oresteia* and the *Odyssey* relate myths of the Mycenaean period, an era of Greek history circa 1600–1200 BC.[44] One of the major events during the Myce-

---

40 Simon Goldhill *Aeschylus, the Oresteia*, 2nd ed. (Cambridge, UK; New York: Cambridge University Press, 2004), vii (hereinafter abbreviated as Goldhill 2004).

41 *Agamemnon* tells the story of King Agamemnon's murder upon his return to Argos from the Trojan War, at the hands of his wife Clytemnestra and her lover Aegisthus (Aeschylus, *Agamemnon*, trans. Hugh Lloyd-Jones (Englewood Cliffs, NJ: Prentice-Hall, 1970). *The Libation Bearers* recounts how Orestes, Agamemnon's and Clytemnestra's son, murdered his mother and her lover to avenge his father's death, after which the Erinyes arrive and Orestes flees (Aeschylus, *The Libation Bearers*, trans. Hugh Lloyd-Jones (Englewood Cliffs, NJ: Prentice-Hall, 1970; hereinafter abbreviated as *The Libation Bearers*). The *Eumenides* tells how Orestes stands before a court established by Athena (Aeschylus, *The Eumenides*, trans. Hugh Lloyd-Jones (Englewood Cliffs, NJ: Prentice-Hall, 1970; hereinafter abbreviated as *Eumenides*).

42 Generative narratives are part of a "narrative map," which traces the scope of the narrative's influence in the field of law and the way in which law and narrative are interwoven. See Almog 2002.

43 Martin Ostwald, *From Popular Sovereignty to the Sovereignty of Law: Law, Society, and Politics in Fifth-Century Athens* (Berkeley: University of California Press, 1986), xx (hereinafter abbreviated as: Ostwald 1986).

44 Irad Malkin, *The Returns of Odysseus: Colonization and Ethnicity* (Berkeley: University of California Press, 1998; hereinafter abbreviated at Malkin, *The Returns*). The Mycenaean Period cor-

naean period, as in Greek mythology generally, was the Trojan War. The *Iliad* and the *Odyssey*, which are attributed to the blind bard Homer, were composed several centuries later, apparently circa 750 BC.[45] The *Oresteia* was written by Aeschylus in 458 BC,[46] several years after a major reform was instituted by the Athenian leader Ephialtes, apparently in 462 BC, concerning the authority of the Areopagite Council, which served as the judicial body of the Athenian *polis*. Due to concerns regarding the Council's extensive authority, its powers were curtailed, and its judicial authority was restricted to cases of premeditated homicide.[47]

The roots of jurisprudence can be traced to the judicial practices represented in the Greek epics relating to the myth of the Trojan War, hundreds of years before Ephialtes' reform and the staging of the *Oresteia*. In the *Iliad*, Book XVIII, the sea nymph Thetis asks Hephaestus to create a shield for her son Achilles. Hephaestus forges a shield on which the entirety of human life is engraved. One of the scenes on the shield depicts a judicial proceeding and shows a judge delivering a verdict in a dispute between two people related to the murder of a third.[48] Homer's description of the scene plays no direct role in advancing the narrative of the *Iliad*. Its purpose is to glorify the shield, but what emerges from this episode is that some type of judicial procedure already existed in the Heroic Age. According to the *Iliad*, the legal proceeding depicted on the shield aroused public interest and drew a large audience, and was conducted in accordance with formal poetics.[49]

The resolution of a murder case by the combined means of payment of retribution and some type of judicial proceeding is thus represented in the myth and depicted in the *Iliad*. Against this backdrop, the question arises as to why the *Odyssey* makes no mention of a possible judicial resolution to a crisis situation, and such potential opens up only many generations later in the *Oresteia*, as a revolutionary innovation instituted by Athena. This question is underscored by

---

responds to what is known in Greek mythology as the Heroic Age. This is one of the five stages of humanity's existence, moving gradually from a starting point of quasi-divine existence to human existence that entails evil and pain. The Heroic Age comes after the Bronze Age and prior to the Iron Age, according to Hesiod, *The Works and Days: Theogony. The Shield of Herakles*, trans. Richmond Lattimore (Ann Arbor: University of Michigan Press, 1959), 15–117.

45 Finley 1972, 47.

46 Goldhill 2004, vii–viii.

47 Goldhill 2004, 8.

48 *Iliad* 18.580–592.

49 For the definition of formal and non-formal legal poetics, see Almog 2002, 42–54.

the similarities between the conflicts at the heart of these tales. Both the *Odyssey* and the *Oresteia* describe a situation that can be termed a crisis of revenge.

Let us begin with the *Odyssey*. After killing all his wife's suitors and maid-servants, Odysseus visits his father Laertes, and informs him of the recent events. Laertes, who is all too familiar with the dynamics of a blood feud, tells his son:

> Oh, but now my heart quakes with fear that all the Ithacans will come down on us in a pack, at any time, and rush the alarm through every island town! (*Odyssey* 24.390–393)

Laertes' premonitions materialize. The slain suitors' families gather around Odysseus' palace with the intention of avenging the deaths of their loved ones. Eupeithes, whose son Antinous was the first to fall at Odysseus' sword, cites the duty of revenge:

> Or we'll hang our heads forever, all disgraced, even by generations down the years, if we don't punish the murderers of our brothers and sons! [...] (*Odyssey* 24.471).

The crowd ignores the warnings of the destructive consequences of vengeance, and prepares to attack. The crisis of revenge reaches its peak.

Just as in the *Odyssey* the relatives of the murdered suitors are compelled to take revenge, in the *Oresteia* it is the Erinyes – the Furies – who seek revenge against Orestes who murdered his mother. When they are deprived of the ability to do so, they threaten to escalate the conflict:

> [...] in requital for my grief from my heart I shall discharge a distillation for the land intolerable; and after that a canker, blasting leaves and children (*Eumenides* 783–785).

In both works, the crisis of revenge poses a threat to the entire public, and in both cases the crisis of revenge is resolved. The *Odyssey* ends as "Athena handed down her pacts of peace between both sides for all the years to come" (*Odyssey* 24.595–598), while the final lines of the *Oresteia* are: "Raise a glad cry, echoing our song! There shall be peace forever [...] for the citizens of Pallas" (*Eumenides* 1043–1045). The similarity between the crises of revenge in both cases underscores the distinct resolution that emerged in each case. In the *Oresteia*, the hero murders his mother and her lover and stands trial for his actions; in the *Odyssey* the hero murders his wife's suitors and the maidservants, is reunited with his family, and is not accountable to any authority for his actions.

Hundreds of years after law gained certain status and presence in Greek society and even artistic representation in the *Iliad*, in the *Odyssey* Homer chooses a law-less conclusion to the crisis of revenge. And hundreds of years after that, in the *Oresteia*, Aeschylus recounts events that happened historically prior to those described in the *Odyssey*, yet presents a generative legal narrative as the resolution of the crisis of revenge at the climax of the story.

Following Michael Bakhtin's notion of the great time, I will delineate the continuum between the *Odyssey* and the *Oresteia*, associating them both to the idea of law and the rule of law. Bakhtin describes a continuous temporal flow of past and future alongside a literary work:

> A work of literature [...] is revealed primarily in the differentiated unity of culture of the epoch in which it is created, but it cannot be closed off in this epoch: its fullness is revealed only in great time.[50]

The *Odyssey* and the *Iliad*, both products of orally related myths, describe the social life and moral values of early Greek society grounded in social rules and norms (including the norm of retaliation) and the role of the Council of Elders, which functioned as a quasi-jury and handled infractions of these rules.[51] As Homer's narrative reveals, the desire to avoid social disgrace was instrumental in guiding social behavior: Homer's work reflects the institutionalization of this norm, where avengers act under the aegis of social sanction[52] and a person whose honor was challenged was obligated to avenge their honor in order to avoid social disgrace.[53] This social regulation also included the option of a "blood price" – an arrangement in which the injurer pays compensation to the injured party in exchange for the latter's renunciation of his right of revenge. In such a case, failure to exercise the duty of revenge generates no loss of social status.[54]

The judicial-like scene engraved upon the shield of Achilles is of central importance in this context, illustrating the norms that already existed at the time to control the urge of vengeance. The shield is the topic of wide-ranging polemics, with diverse, sometimes contradictory interpretations of almost each and every one of Homer's lines.[55] One approach sees the shield's scene as a representation of the juridification of revenge. According to this view, the scene is a depiction of

---

50 Michael Bakhtin, *Speech Genres and Other Late Essays*, trans. Vern W. McGee, eds. Caryl Emerson and Michael Holquis (Austin: University of Texas Press, 1986), 5.
51 Eva Cantarella, "Private Revenge and Public Justice: The Settlement of Disputes in Homer's Iliad," *Punishment & Society* 3.4 (2001): 473–483, 478–479 (hereinafter abbreviated as: Cantarella 2001).
52 Cantarella 2001, 479.
53 Cantarella 2001, 475.
54 Cantarella 2001, 477.
55 See Raymond Westbrook, "The Trial Scene in the Iliad," *Harvard Studies in Classical Philology* 94 (1992): 53–76, 76.

a "blood price" arrangement gone awry, requiring a public resolution of the disputants' claims.[56] But even if the exact details of the dispute remain vague, the fact that Homer chose to describe the scene marks it as a representation of "a crucial moment in legal history: the moment of transition when a system of revenge gives way to a system of criminal law."[57]

Despite the interpretative differences of opinion surrounding the shield, it constitutes evidence that a system of conflict resolution already existed in Homeric society, which preluded the era of the *polis:* The disputants submit their conflict to external resolution; they voice their claims in a public forum, in accordance with a known, formal, public procedure.[58] Michael Gagarin, who extensively analyzed quasi-judicial situations in Greek literature predating the *Oresteia*, notes that the later judicial scene that appears in the *Oresteia* also begins with two parties who submit their conflict before an authoritative body (the goddess Athena), who then decides to establish a court, similarly to the scene described upon the shield of Achilles. The innovation that is presented by means of the judicial procedure in the *Oresteia*, then, is not so revolutionary.[59]

Returning to the *Odyssey*, it is interesting to note the abundance of references to the injured party's duty to take revenge on the injurer in order to preserve their honor. In the *Odyssey*, the crisis of revenge peaks in the decision by the slain suitors' relatives to avenge the latter's deaths in order to avoid disgrace. Here, then, we see revenge not as an uncontrollable personal impulse but as a regulating social norm, a component of the existing social order known to all. In light of what we know from the scene upon the shield in the *Iliad*, this social order makes it possible to contain revenge with no further bloodshed and may involve the exercise of judicial authority under certain conditions.

This is the view of David Luban, who holds that whereas the *Oresteia* is the birth-site of judicial instrumentalism, Homer's work (alongside that of Hesiod) marks, for the first time in Western civilization, a preoccupation with the role of legal justice in establishing social order.[60] Finley too emphasizes the innovation of the *Odyssey* in this context. Whereas in the *Iliad* personal motivations

---

56 Cantarella 2001, 478–479.

57 Cantarella 2001, 480.

58 Michael Gagarin, *Early Greek Law* (Berkeley, CA: University of California Press, 1986), 19, 27 (hereinafter abbreviated as Gagarin 1986).

59 Gagarin 1986, 41.

60 David Luban, *Legal Modernism* (Ann Arbor: University of Michigan Press, 1997), 298 (hereinafter abbreviated as: Luban 1997).

reign supreme, in the *Odyssey* the personal element is complemented by "the demands of justice [...] even if only partially and crudely."[61]

Indeed, the *Odyssey* reflects endorsement of the notion of social life regulated by binding rules already in its opening lines:

> Sing to me of the man, Muse, the man of twists and turns driven time and again off course, once he had plundered the hallowed heights of Troy.
> Many cities of men he saw and learned their minds, many pains he suffered, heartsick on the open sea, fighting to save his life and bring his comrades home. But he could not save them from disaster, hard as he strove – the recklessness of their own ways destroyed them all, the blind fools, they devoured the cattle of the Sun and the Sungod blotted out he day of their return. (*Odyssey* 1.1–11)

The story of the oxen itself appears later in Book XII of the *Odyssey*. Odysseus and his men arrive at the island where the oxen of Helios, the sun god, are grazing. Odysseus informs his men of the norm prohibiting any harm to the oxen, and demands that they pledge an oath to honor it, but in his absence, their hunger drives them to slaughter some of the oxen. Zeus accepts Helios' demand to avenge the killing of his oxen, and all those who violated the norm are drowned. Only Odysseus, who abided by the norm, is spared. The choice to set this relatively marginal episode at the very beginning of the *Odyssey* points to its significance. The episode highlights the leitmotif of just retribution, which extends throughout the work.

Immediately after the opening lines that manifest the idea of recompense, in Book I, *Athena & Telemachos*, Homer uses a quasi-legal framing to describe the gods' gathering on Mt. Olympus to discuss the matter of Odysseus. The scene is organized in a way that recalls a judicial proceeding, and Athena assumes a role similar to an advocate representing a client. Conscious of the adversarial nature of the deliberations, she exploits the absence of Poseidon, who is hostile to her "client," to advocate Odysseus' cause, requesting a decision that would facilitate his return home.

In the ensuing debate, the scales indeed tip in favor of Odysseus, mainly due to the sympathetic position of Zeus, who serves as a kind of head of court and supports the ideas of justice, retribution, and due recompense for loyalty. Zeus enumerates Odysseus' merits:

---

61 Finley 1972, 37. See in this context also the approach presented by Aleardo Zanghellini, "The Foundations of the Rule of Law," *Yale Journal of Law & the Humanities* 28.2 (2016): 213–240, 228: "in the Odyssey rule of law concerns coagulate with particular insistence around the management of guest-host relationships: specifically, ignorance and/or violation of the duties and rites of hospitality toward strangers" (hereinafter abbreviated as: Zanghellini 2016).

> Now, how on earth could I forget Odysseus? Great Odysseus who excels all men in wisdom, excels in offerings too he gives the immortal gods who rule the vaulting skies? (*Odyssey* 1.78–80)

Yet he also presents the counter-argument, Poseidon's understandable anger at Odysseus for having blinded his son. In the same breath, though, Zeus dismisses Poseidon's position as a minority opinion that is overridden by the majority:

> But come, all of us here put heads together now,
> work out his journey home so Odysseus can return.
> Lord Poseidon, I trust, will let his anger go.
> How can he stand his ground against the will
> of all the gods at once – one god alone? (*Odyssey* 1.91–96).

Homer frames this Olympian council as a quasi-judicial body that issues an operative ruling. The debate ends with Athena's enrollment in the mission of arranging Odysseus' return to Ithaca.

The Olympian council's decision to grant Odysseus a "right of return" is confirmed in Book V, which describes another divine gathering, again without Poseidon. Here too, the council convenes, and Athena continues to represent Odysseus' interests resolutely and effectively. Having succeeded in obtaining a favorable decision at the earlier meeting, she now focuses on advancing its practical implementation. She mentions the danger to Telemachus, whom the suitors are threatening to kill, and the urgency of sending Odysseus, stranded on the nymph Calypso's island, on his way. Zeus instructs her to put the plan of return into action, and Hermes informs Calypso of the decision: "Now Zeus commands you to send him off with all good speed" (*Odyssey* 5.125).

Calypso, however, opposes the decision, arguing that she earned the *right* to hold Odysseus by saving him from drowning and taking care of him. Calypso's position is rejected. When Hermes warns her not to protest too forcefully, she acknowledges the authority of the Olympian ruling and sends Odysseus on his way. Angry Poseidon complicates Odysseus' journey, but he too, like Calypso, accepts the verdict of the Olympian tribunal. The *Odyssey* is fundamentally the detailed description of the execution of this quasi-judicial decision adopted by the gods in council, which is presented as being in accord with the principle of justice.

Further allusions to law, glorification of social life subjugated to the rule of law, and condemnation of lawless individuals are introduced through the depictions of three societies visited by Odysseus in the course of his long journey home: the island of the Cyclopes, the land of the Phaeacians, and Ithaca. Each reflects a distinct social order.

In Book IX, Odysseus tells his Phaeacian hosts the tale of his confrontation with the Cyclopes. The first thing he had asked himself upon arriving on the Cyclopean shores, he recounts, was whether he would meet law-abiding folks or their opposite:

> I'll go across with my own ship and crew and probe the natives living over there. What are they–violent, savage, lawless? or friendly to strangers, god-fearing men? (*Odyssey* 9.194 – 196)

The answer is soon discovered. He and his companions enter the cave of the Cyclops Polyphemus, in order to exchange gifts as guests, as demanded by Greek custom.[62] The Cyclops, however, flout this norm by devouring Odysseus' men. In an act of deception, Odysseus manages to escape with some of his group by blinding the Cyclops with a wooden stake. The absence of law is a central theme in this story. Polyphemus and the other Cyclopes are referred to as lawless brutes (*Odyssey* 9.120) and Odysseus repeatedly emphasizes that the Cyclopes as a group are characterized by the total absence of rule of law.

> They have no meeting place for council, no laws either,
> no, up on the mountain peaks they live in arching caverns
> each a law to himself, ruling his wives and children,
> not a care in the world for any neighbor (*Odyssey* 9.125 – 128).

The Cyclopes' disregard of law is further highlighted against the contrast to the highly civilized Phaeacians, in whose land Odysseus finds himself in Book IX, following his misadventures with the Cyclopes. Their social existence is described as utopian in nature.

An assembly of Phaeacians listens to Odysseus' plea for help. In the course of the event one of the Phaeacians, Euryalus, is disrespectful toward Odysseus and the king rules that the offender owes Odysseus an apology and a gift. Euryalus accepts the verdict gracefully and complies. Indeed, it seems that the Phaeacian society resolves disputes and conflicts peacefully. The king describes himself as someone who never gets angry and believes that moderation is always best. Everyone respects the queen for her good intelligence. After hearing the detailed stories of Odysseus' travels, and after hosting him generously and plying him with gifts, the Phaeacians urge their king to send the guest back home.

According to one approach, Phaeacian society is depicted as being preoccupied with games, pleasures, and niceties of manners – at the expense of

---

62 Finley 1972, 83 – 85.

obedience to customary governmental duties. As a result, it is difficult to distinguish the king from his subjects. The king recounts how his authority was dismantled in favor of collective decision-making.[63] However, the Homeric narrator does not appear to be critical of Phaeacian social and governmental order, and describes their land in striking contrast to that of the Cyclopes, inasmuch as it concerns the subjugation of the individual to the social order. As Aleardo Zanghellini describes, both societies – the Phaeacian and the Cyclopesian – represent a "formula, repeated throughout the epic, [that] consolidates the association between, on the one hand, lawlessness and savagery and, on the other hand, between legality and the qualities of being friendly to strangers and god-fearing."[64]

Ithaca, Odysseus' homeland, exemplifies a third model of social order. In principle, Ithaca has a well-defined social order. As described in Book II, Odysseus' son Telemachus seeks to invoke the existing customs to rectify the wrongful state of affairs caused by the suitors. However, his request to convene an assembly is rejected on grounds of the procedural argument that only certain matters, such as an enemy at the city's gate or a weighty public issue, justify such an assembly. Telemachus admits to his personal distress, caused by the actions of the suitors, the uninvited guests who are wasting his property, and appeals to the assembly:

> I beg you by Olympian Zeus, by Themis too,
> who sets assemblies free and calls us into session –
> stop, my friends! (*Odyssey* 2.73–75)

Telemachus' appeal refers to the suitors' violation of longstanding customs in Homeric society. Indeed, part of what has gone wrong in Ithaca during Odysseus' absence is the blatant disregard of the customs and principles to which Telemachus refers. Antinous, one of the suitors, openly rejects Telemachus' right to address the assembly, issuing a threatening demand:

> We'll not go back
> to our old estates or leave for other parts,
> not till she weds the Argive man she fancies. (*Odyssey* 2.142–143).

---

63 Jasper Griffin, *Homer, The Odyssey*, 2nd ed. (Cambridge: Cambridge University Press, 2004), 85 (hereinafter abbreviated as: Griffin 2004).
64 Zanghellini 2016, 231.

Despite Mentor's support, Telemachus fails to win the assembly over to his side, and the suitors continue their depredations. All Telemachus can do is to warn the suitors that those who transgress the norms will ultimately be punished, in words that precisely foretell the future:

> But I'll cry out to the everlasting gods in hopes
> that Zeus will pay you back with a vengeance – all of you
> destroyed in my house while I go scot-free myself! (*Odyssey* 2.161–163)

This protest reflects the principle of accountability, known to the poet and his audience: Transgressors are accountable for their transgressions. Raising the subject of accountability for the suitors' impending deaths at the beginning of the story, the poet already anticipates that no one will bear responsibility for these deaths, with which the story will end. The main point here is that accountability for their deaths is discussed explicitly, and where there is no belief in accountability, there will be no need for careful planning or divine support to structure an exemption.

There is no clear delineation of the "constitutional" state of affairs in Ithaca as regards monarchical succession.[65] But even in light of this lacuna, Ithaca of the *Odyssey* appears to be a society with practices that are in general affinity with what is now broadly regarded as public law. In principle, social institutions such as a people's assembly function. The suitors, despite their long and upsetting stay in Ithaca, do not use violence but rather concentrate their efforts on persuading the queen to choose one of them. Recognition of property rights and the custom of gifts bring to mind practices that today would be generally grasped as echoing private law. Practices that are commonly identified with criminal law, such as acknowledgment of the principles of accountability, guilt and punishment also exist in Ithaca, but were seriously weakened during Odysseus' prolonged absence, as reflected by the suitors' conduct. Odysseus' reaction and his slaughter of the suitors lead toward the crisis of revenge. At the height of the crisis, the aged Halitherses reminds the suitors' relatives, who are poised to attack Odysseus, of the fundamental principles of the social order and the suitors' responsibility for its disruption:

> Hear me, men of Ithaca. Hear what I have to say.
> Thanks to your own craven hearts these things were done!
> You never listened to me or the good commander Mentor,
> you never put a stop to your sons' senseless folly.

---

65 Griffin 2004, 85.

What fine work they did, so blind, so reckless,
carving away the wealth, affronting the wife
of a great and famous man, telling themselves
that he'd return no more! So let things rest now.
Listen to me for once – I say don't attack!
Else some will draw the lightning on their necks (*Odyssey* 24.501–510).

His words fall on deaf ears, and it is only Odysseus' return and his violent actions that finally repair the disruption and restore social order. After the situation has been rectified, all those involved in the crisis of revenge revert to the pattern of ordinary social existence.

The *Odyssey*, then, does not describe an experience or space devoid of law. The phenomenon of law is manifest in multiple contexts. Although the crisis of revenge that ends the *Odyssey* is not resolved by a judicial procedure, it does not lack a legal dimension. A social agreement – the signing of pacts of peace for years to come – ultimately resolves the dispute, and that is the bottom line, even if preceded by Athena's intervention, *deus ex machina*.

A return to the social order is devised not only by Athena's intervention and the divine amnesia she casts upon those seeking revenge, but is also the result of an intricate resolution of a local power struggle. The king's absence, his son's youth and inexperience, and the queen's decision to resist the pressures placed upon her inevitably ignited a struggle over the political control and leadership of Ithaca. The crisis of revenge in the *Odyssey* is only one element in this struggle and, in fact, is its last gasp. Upon Odysseus' triumphant return and recapture of the reins of power and rule in Ithaca, and under Athena's guidance, all parties are able to achieve a closure of the crisis through agreement and mutual acceptance of the preceding events.

In contrast, in the *Oresteia* the crisis of revenge is of another type, and its exceptional circumstances call for a different resolution. That requirement is satisfied by the judicial procedure instituted by Athena, a procedure that would have been narratively incongruent in the *Odyssey*.

Paths Leading Toward Generative Legal Narrative

Notions pertaining to law in the *Odyssey* and the *Oresteia* can be ascribed to various factors, such as the development of the concept of justice in the centuries between the writing of the two works and the personal poetic choices of their respective authors. Aeschylus was predisposed to producing a detailed account of the establishment of a court in the *Oresteia*, while Homer chose to focus on other elements of his stories.[66] Both personal imagination and the period-specific cultural patterns in the era in which the work was written are of central importance. In addition, I find three factors – poetic, performative, and sociopolitical – that may explain why a generative legal narrative appears in Aeschylus' work but not in Homer's.[67]

I begin by briefly introducing the poetics of epics, tragedy, and law. Poetics is an array of principles referring to the nature and essence of literary expression and the ways in which it creates meaning.[68] The earliest theory of poetics is found in Aristotle's *Poetics*, written circa mid-fourth century BC, an effort to systematically describe the tools through which a literary text elicits (or fails to elicit) responses in its audience. Aristotle, who regarded poetics as the art of mimicry and representation (*mimesis*), mainly discussed tragedy, although he did refer to other genres, including epic and comedy. To Aristotle, "epic" meant the Homeric epics – the *Iliad* and the *Odyssey*.[69]

According to Aristotle, the poetics of the epics differs from the poetics of tragedy in several respects: epic paints upon a broader canvas multiple episodes that form a web of narratives. As a result, epic poetry may include counter-logical elements,[70] and is denser than tragedy: "any Epic poem will furnish subjects for several tragedies."[71] But the breadth of the canvas on which epic poetry draws makes no concessions with respect to a distinctive narrative core:

> Thus the story of the Odyssey can be stated briefly. A certain man is absent from home for many years; he is jealously watched by Poseidon, and left desolate. Meanwhile his home is in a wretched plight – suitors are wasting his substance and plotting against his son. At length, tempest-tossed, he himself arrives; he makes certain persons acquainted with

---

66 E.g., complex narrative twists, and numerous poetic digressions that produce various subplots and give space to many minor characters.

67 For a general discussion of Greek drama's social, aesthetic and psychological dimensions, see Jean-Pierre Vernant and Pierre Vidal-Naquet, *Myth and Tragedy in Ancient Greece*, trans. Janet Loyd (Sussex: Harvester Press, 1981), viii–ix (hereinafter abbreviated as: Vernant and Vial-Naquet 1981).

68 See C. Hugh Holman and William Harmon, *A Handbook to Literature*, 6th ed. (New York: Macmillan, 1992), 364 (hereinafter abbreviated as: Holman and Harmon 1992).

69 Holman and Harmon 1992, 114.

70 For details of these differences, see Holman and Harmon 1992, 115.

71 Aristotle, *The Poetics of Aristotle*, ed. and trans. Samuel Henry Butcher, 3rd ed. (London; New York: Macmillan, 1992). (hereinafter abbreviated as *The Poetics of Aristotle*, Butcher trans), 111.

him; he attacks the suitors with his own hand, and is himself preserved while he destroys them. This is the essence of the plot; the rest is episode.[72]

Homer, Aristotle tells us, is as an outstanding craftsman who carefully considers the flow of the narrative. Accordingly, "Homer did not include all the adventures of Odysseus [...] but he made the Odyssey [...] to center around an action that in our sense of the word is one."[73] Into this "one action," focused exclusively on Odysseus' successful return home, integration of a contending story of substance about the establishment of legal justice – a story that takes center-stage in the *Oresteia* – is hardly feasible. The story of the *Odyssey* remains focused on Odysseus' belated but successful return, and is conveyed via a dense and precise epic tapestry that leaves little room for a narrative thread extensively describing a judicial procedure. In contrast, the establishment of legal justice has consequences for all of society, and as the *Eumenides* illustrates, time and again it shifts the spotlight from the individual (Orestes) to the polis and its future.

The epic pulse reaches its peak in the *Odyssey*'s concluding Book. The dead suitors go their way to the Halls of Death, where they encounter the ghosts of Achilles and Agamemnon. Agamemnon recounts Achilles' glorious death on the battlefield, as opposed to his own ignominious demise. At the same time, Odysseus visits his father Laertes who is terrified of the vengeance of the suitors' families, even though he believes that the killing of the suitors was justified and that the suitors had to pay for their reckless deeds.

Meanwhile, word of the suitors' deaths has spread throughout the city, and an angry crowd gathered around the palace. Eupeithes, whose son was the first victim, tells the crowd that Odysseus brought disaster to the entire public: he led many to Troy, lost men and ships, and upon his return killed the finest of the land. Revenge is necessary to avoid eternal shame, Eupeithes concludes. Medon, whose life had been spared by Odysseus not long before, offers the following argument: Odysseus could not have succeeded without assistance from the gods, and therefore attacking him would lead to devastation. He is supported by Halitherses, who reminds everyone that the suitors committed a great wrongdoing. The crowd remains unconvinced and prepares to attack Odysseus. At that moment, Athena accosts her father Zeus and requests his intervention:

> Will you prolong the pain, the cruel fighting here
> Or hand down pacts of peace between both sides? (*Odyssey* 24.536 – 526).

---

72 *The Poetics of Aristotle*, Butcher trans., 65.
73 *The Poetics of Aristotle*, Butcher trans., 33 – 35.

Zeus replies:

> let both sides seal their pacts that he shall reign for life,
> and let us purge their memories of the bloody slaughter
> of their brothers and their sons. Let them be friends,
> devoted as in the old days. Let peace and wealth
> come cresting through the land (*Odyssey* 24.527–538).

Before the proposed amnesia can take effect, Odysseus hurries to the scene of the impending battle and there, with Athena's help, he slays Eupeithes, leader of the calls for revenge. Odysseus and his son prepare to take on their remaining foes, but at this juncture Athena appears in full glory, ordering the disputants to desist from hostilities. Although they initially obey her, Odysseus has second thoughts and attempts to attack again. Zeus casts a smoke-shrouded bolt of lightning, and Athena again orders Odysseus to call a halt, warning him of Zeus' wrath if he fails to lay down his arms. Odysseus finally complies. Assuming the appearance and voice of Mentor, Athena strikes an alliance between the two sides for the time to come.

This narrative density, which includes events simultaneously occurring in several spaces and contexts, creates a hectic conclusion to the crisis of revenge in the *Odyssey*. The accelerated pace, which brings to mind the picaresque novel,[74] is unlikely to give rise to precise, detailed preoccupation with the careful establishment of a court and a judicial procedure. The *Odyssey* presents the world of myth, a world that is "chaotic, full of contradictions, impossible versions, adaptations and fabrications."[75] Odysseus' confrontation with the suitors is the final station along his turbulent journey that includes charged encounters with monsters, goddesses, Sirens, Cyclopes, and others. The focus throughout remains on Odysseus' journey and impeded return home. This direction is unlikely to accommodate a competing detailed account of the establishment of judicial procedure, which could become the heart of the narrative, as in the story crafted by Aeschylus in the *Oresteia*.

In contrast, the *Eumenides* leads gradually and consistently from the inception of the crisis of revenge toward its resolution by means of the establishment of legal justice. Both before and after the establishment of the court, the protagonists engage in adversarial discussions and debates. The Erinyes and Apollo, Orestes and Athena, and Athena and the Erinyes advance arguments and coun-

---

74 As suggested by Adorno and Horkheimer in Theodor W. Adorno and Max Horkheimer, *Dialectic of Enlightenment*, trans. John Cumming (London: Verso, 1997), 46 (hereinafter abbreviated as: Adorno and Horkheimer 1997).
75 Malkin 1998, 29.

terarguments negotiating the question of Orestes' fate using desertist rhetoric saturated with references to law, justice, and judging. Already at the beginning of the play, Apollo, who agrees to take Orestes under his protecting wing, directs him "to the city of Pallas" (*Eumenides* 79) where a legal resolution of his quandary awaits:

> And there shall we have judges of your cause, and words to charm them, and shall discover means to release you forever from this distress (*Eumenides* 81–83).

Orestes adopts Apollo's judicial rhetoric and immediately upon arriving at Athena's temple he does not ask for mercy, but demands to be put on trial:

> I come to your house; your image, goddess. Will I guard here as I await the issue of the trial? (*Eumenides* 242–243)

As soon as Athena becomes involved, she too employs judicial rhetoric. After the Erinyes state their demands, she asks whether they are willing to accept her judicial verdict: "Would you commit to the settlement of the charge?" (*Eumenides* 434) and is answered: "Surely, we reverence you as worthy and of worthy parentage" (*Eumenides* 435). After some further exchanges with Orestes, he reiterates his demand for her verdict: "Whether I acted justly or unjustly, you decide the case! For however I may fare, I shall rest content with your decision" (*Eumenides* 468–469). The foundation thus having been laid, and after further consideration of the issue of authority, Athena proclaims the establishment of a human court as the only way out of the dilemma:

> The matter is harder than any mortal thinks to judge of; it is not right even for me to decide a trial for murder that brings down fierce wrath; [...] But since this matter has devolved on me [...] judges [...] of murder, respecting the covenant of their oaths, which I shall establish for all time [...] I will select the best among my citizens, and will return, to decide this issue in all sincerity. (*Eumenides* 470–488)

The *Eumenides* describes progress toward this climax through its references to adjudication, which leads naturally to Athena's festive proclamation of the establishment of a court and the civilian duty to maintain and protect it. The background to the implementation of a formal judicial procedure and its focal artistic and public role is built up gradually from the beginning of the play. In other words, the poetic choices in the *Oresteia* pave the way toward the establishment of legal justice.

Let me now support my argument by illustrating the resemblance between tragedy and legal proceeding as spectacles. The generative legal narrative constructed by Aeschylus is based on a powerful presentation of a legal proceeding as a spectacle. The *Eumenides* is a detailed account of the transfer of divine authority to human responsibility, and an exemplar of how the judicial spectacle should be conducted.

The nature of the stage created by Aeschylus makes a detailed description of the judicial procedure not only possible but also natural. As we learn from Aristotle, Aeschylus introduced significant innovations to the staging of tragedy: "Aeschylus first introduced a second actor; he diminished the importance of the Chorus, and assigned the leading part to the dialogue."[76] These innovations, recognized throughout history, mark the transition from monologue to dialogue and gave rise to drama as we know it today. Hundreds of years after Aeschylus' death, he is mentioned by the Roman poet Horace in *Ars Poetica*, a work dedicated to artistic expression. Reviewing the history of the tragic form, Horace first mentions Thespis, "said to have invented a new kind of tragedy," accompanied by novel visual effects – "and to have carried his pieces about in carts, which [certain strollers], who had their faces besmeared with lees of wine, sang and acted."[77] He then turns to address Aeschylus' performative innovations:

> After him Aeschylus, the inventor of the vizard mask and decent robe, laid the stage over with boards of a tolerable size, and taught to speak in lofty tone, and strut in the buskin.[78]

Law, too, uses linguistic and visual formats, texts and images, to signal that the decision reached in court is due and apposite. These poetic tools are necessary to achieve this effect and they are implemented in two arenas – the visual and the verbal – through practices that I have proposed calling *formal poetics* and *informal poetics*.[79] These practices shape the form and content of judicial procedures, as well as the spaces in which they transpire.

---

76 *The Poetics of Aristotle*, Butcher trans. 19. Some speculate that Aeschylus himself may have participated in the *Oresteia* as an actor. See C. W. Marshall, "Casting the Oresteia," *The Classical Journal* 98.3 (2003): 257–274, 258.

77 Horace, *Ars Poetica*, at *Poetry Foundation* website (Adapted from translations by C. Smart and E. H. Blakeney, *Horace on the Art of Poetry* (London: Scholartis Press, 1928) available at https://www.poetryfoundation.org/articles/69381/ars-poetica (hereinafter abbreviated as: Horace *Ars Poetica*),

78 Horace, *Ars Poetica*.

79 As I have noted in another context, "the rules of legal procedure are in a sense formal instructions for creating meaningful representations. Beside this system of formal rules another system operates which is not anchored in positive directives and can be described as an informal poetic system. The combined operation of both systems determines how the law appears, is heard and grasped." (Almog 2002)

The most important representation of doing justice is the adversarial procedure – two sides argue before the bench, according to known rules, in an event that is unrepeatable, though it echoes familiar formats. For the judicial procedure to constitute an efficient representation of doing justice, it must convince its addressees that its methods are fair and to this end, it harnesses the element of visibility. The judges' solemn entry into the courtroom, which serves as a stage, and the audience's rising to receive them are markers of the place and time in which justice is done. The judicial procedure is thus simultaneously both a mechanism and a representation of doing justice.

This is the stage that Aeschylus designs when constructing the first act of judicial justice in history. Visibility is an integral component of the judicial procedure, and Aeschylus was active at a time when the performative tradition made it possible *to display* a procedure. The establishment of the first court and rule of law requires a visual representation of certain complexity. The spectacle of the court in the *Oresteia* illustrates and manifests the public nature of the procedure, the basic principle that ensures its fairness and correctness and at the same time expresses the vital link between seeing and doing justice. At the same time, Aeschylus' text, which refers to the contents of the judicial procedure conducted by Athena, alludes to the formal and informal verbal poetics that structure the adversarial judicial procedure.

Upon summoning the judges, who are expected to commit to "respecting the covenant of their oaths, which I shall establish for all time" (*Eumenides* 483 – 484), Athena goes into detail, establishing not only the obligatory nature of the judicial procedure from now onwards, but also how it will be conducted. In effect, she establishes the poetics of procedure that serves society to this day:

> Do you summon witnesses and proofs, sworn evidence to assist justice (*Eumenides* 485 – 486)

and proceeds to describe the procedure's public features:

> Make proclamation, herald and bid the people to their places! And let the shrill Tyrrhenian trumpet filled with human breath show to the people its high-pitched note! For this court is filled, it is proper that silence be kept [...] (*Eumenides* 566 – 571).

Athena goes on to conduct the debate in an adversarial manner, giving the disputants an opportunity to have their say. After a public count of the judges' votes, and a declaration, also public, of her decision in favor of the defendant, the procedure reaches its climax with the court's announcement: "This man stands acquitted on the charge of murder" (*Eumenides* 751).

Aeschylus creates nothing less than a novel representation of the judicial spectacle. Even if judicial activities of various kinds are found in myth, reflected in the epos and practiced in Greek and Athenian society as well, it is Aeschylus who, by means of the poetics that he innovated and perfected, presents a drama that crystallizes these factors into "the rule of law" and connects the rule of law to the judicial performance.[80]

The poetics of tragedy accommodates the legal orientation of the *polis*. According to Jean-Pierre Vernant and Pierre Vidal-Naquet, "Tragedy is not only an art form; it is also a social institution that the city [...] set up alongside its political and legal institutions."[81] Tragedy, then, brings to the stage not only "an ancient heroic legend"[82] but also an emergent contemporary institution – a court of law. It is the form of the tragedy that enables the construction of a new bridge between the mythical traditions embodied in the epos and the new forms of legal practices.

The aesthetic principles of performative expression allow Aeschylus to create a representation of the transition to a procedural era. The grandeur of the stage fashioned by Aeschylus, with its revolutionary number of actors and their prominent costumes, brings to mind the power of the judicial spectacle and the formal and informal poetics employed in it.[83] The development of the poetics of dramatic performance than, converges with the honing of the poetics of the judicial spectacle.[84]

Finally, it is helpful to elucidate the fertile correspondence between the political shift in fifth-century BC Athens from tyrannical regimes toward democracy and the poetic transition in Aeschylus' time that provided an apt background for the emergence of a generative legal narrative. Both the *Odyssey* and the *Oresteia* recount events of the Heroic era. While Homer and Aeschylus both are inspired by the distant Achaean period, each operates in a distinct "story time." The developments and transformations that Athenian society underwent over the cen-

---

80 In this context, see Richars Kuhns' description of how Aeschylus uses performance to heighten the status of Athenian jurisprudence. (Richard Kuhns, *The House, the City, and the Judge: the growth of moral awareness in the Oresteia* (Indianapolis: Bobbs-Merrill, 1962), 66 – 67 (hereinafter abbreviated as: Kuhns 1962).

81 Vernant and Vidal-Naquet 1981, 36.

82 Vernant and Vidal-Naquet 1981, 36.

83 Almog 2002.

84 Maria Aristodemou discusses the power of new signifiers to create a reality, including judicial reality: "[a]rtists can use their power to create new signs, and thereby new selves and new laws" (Maria Aristodemou, "The Seduction of Mimesis: Theater as Woman and the Play of Difference and Excess in Aeschylus's 'Oresteia'," *Cardozo Studies in Law and Literature* 11.1 (1999): 1–33, 26).

turies that elapsed between the two works called for the establishment of the rule of law that is reflected in the *Oresteia*.

The Homeric world features a stratified class society, with the spotlight cast mainly on its highborn aristocracy, whose members see themselves demi-gods, the differences (except for the latter's immortality) being "matters of degree, prestige and power."[85] The will of the gods serves as the law, which always prevails: "Their will is just because it is their will."[86] In the Homeric epic, the will of the upper classes similarly serves as the law: "He does not perform his actions because they are just, to the contrary: since he is an aristocrat and owes no account to anyone, his actions are just because he performs them."[87]

The *Oresteia* tells a new story, in which humans waive their autonomy and the power and liberty to freely conduct their affairs. As Simon Goldhill explains, this is first and foremost a political story.[88] The fifth century BC was marked by a social and political transformation, from oligarchical or tyrannical regimes to democracy. In 507 BC, Cleisthenes' reforms established a democratic system.[89] The political upheavals in Athens during those years yielded a vigorous public debate that earned the name "the Fifth Century Enlightenment." The *Oresteia's* appearance when it did was an inseparable part of this process of enlightenment. The *Oresteia* manifests the convergence of the political moment with what Vernant and Vidal-Naquet call "the tragic transition."[90] The tragic transition represents and simultaneously constitutes a symptom of the unresolved tension between two systems of values and ideas when it reaches a peak: This happens when a space opens up at the core of social existence, one broad enough to accommodate the opposition between political and legal thinking on one hand, and mythical and heroic tradition on the other.[91]

Vernant and Vidal-Naquet explain the profound difference between myth and tragedy. Whereas myth, in its original form, provides answers without explicitly formulating the questions, tragedy employs the mythical story to formulate complex questions that remain unanswered.[92] Mythical heroes have a fabulous

---

85 Ailliam K. C. Guthrie, *The Greeks and their Gods* (Boston: Beacon Press, 1955), 121 (hereinafter abbreviated as: Guthrie 1955).

86 Guthrie 1995, 123.

87 Guthrie 1995, 122.

88 Goldhill 2004, 47.

89 Goldhill 2004, 2. In 507 BC, after years of struggle, Cleisthenes' reforms established a democratic system for the first time.

90 Vernant and Vidal-Naquet 1981, 34.

91 Vernant and Vidal-Naquet 1981, 34.

92 Vernant and Vidal-Naquet 1981, 34.

existence. The Homeric epic cleverly "organizes" the mythical experience.[93] The tragic hero originally comes from the same mythical sphere, but the drama implants him in the reality of the fifth-century BC *polis*, riven by political struggles.[94] In effect, the tragic transition leverages the mythical narrative in order to tell a new story that is suited to the reality of the *polis* and its audience.

This complicated turn is exemplified by the figure of Orestes. The references to Orestes in the *Odyssey* express an unequivocal moral directive presented as a model of worthy behavior, who acted rightfully by killing his mother, the murderer of his father. His dilemma is given no expression. In contrast, in the *Oresteia*, Orestes is tormented by doubts: "Pylades, what am I to do? Shall I respect my mother, and not kill her?" (*The Libation Bearers* 899). Discussion of this question and its implications is conducted and developed in multiple discursive arenas, including the judicial, throughout the *Libation Bearers* and the *Eumenides*. The presentation of this discourse is only possible against the background of an extant ethos centering on the rule of law and respect for the law. This was indeed the background in Aeschylus' time, which did not exist in the Homeric age. The convergence of the political moment with the tragic transition in Aeschylus' time created a generative legal narrative for a fully receptive audience capable of charged it with meaning.

The *Odyssey* and the *Oresteia* are performative works: Their creators addressed them to audiences who charged these artistic expressions with meaning by identifying themselves and their values in these accounts. The representation of legal justice in the *Oresteia* is not merely Greek drama's reflection of the transformation of the Athenian judicial system, but also a story told to an audience living in a very different sociopolitical reality from the Homeric era. The poetic expression that changes in response to this reality makes it possible to accommodate the narrative about the establishment of legal justice and the relocation of the ancient law or retaliation from the realm of the personal to the realm of the *polis*, which represents the public.

In summary, the convergence of these three paths – poetic, performative, and sociopolitical – created a juncture potent enough to produce a powerful representation of the moment at which the rule of law emerged.

---

93 Adorno and Horkheimer 1997, 43. On the complex relation between epic and myth in the Homeric oeuvre, see 46–47.
94 Vernant and Vidal-Naquet 1981, 34.

Athena: Multifaceted Goddess-Judge

Twice in the *Odyssey* – once at the beginning of the story and another time toward its conclusion – Zeus remarks that Odysseus' return is the consequence of Athena's wishes and plan.[95] The entire epic is in effect a particularizing of the determined manner in which Athena accomplishes her plan. In the *Eumenides* Athena declares that she will take action to end the dispute "since this matter has devolved on me" (*Eumenides* 482). However, more than the matter devolves on her, it seems that Athena voluntarily takes it upon herself to resolve the matter as she sees fit.

In both works, Athena stands at the center of the conflict, and is motivated by her wish to help her two protégés, Odysseus and Orestes. She resolves the conflict in each case through active intervention, which combines coercion and intimidation with elements of rhetoric, conciliation, and persuasion. There is, however, a significant divergence between her modes of action in the two cases. She assists Odysseus in planning his return and taking revenge on the suitors. Athena promises to be at his side and is true to her word. She operates *ex post* on Orestes' behalf, only after he himself has performed the act of revenge, murdered his mother, and fled to her temple. In the Homeric epos her intervention on behalf of Odysseus is direct and much more intensive, while in Aeschylus' play, Athena establishes a new institution – a court – that is harnessed to solve Orestes' predicament. The difference in the way the two authors describe Athena's modes of action is usually attributed to the social and political developments in Greece in the centuries that separate the works.

Aeschylus' description of Athena's intervention reflects the transformation in which the judicial roles and procedures, already present on the Areopagus, shifted from preservation of patriarchal rituals to pursuit of civil justice in the interest of the polis, that is – the declining authority of the patriarchal family and its subordination to the authority of the *polis*.[96] Interestingly, Athena's character in the *Eumenides* retains prominent features of Homeric Athena. First, in both narratives Athena appears to know that brute power alone – whether through a judicial act or an act of violence – is unable to achieve sustainable solutions in a social environment. In both narratives, Athena relies on more than her mere power to advance an agreement and resolve the crisis of revenge.

---

95 In Book V, he tells her: "For is not this your own intention, as you have counseled it, how Odysseus shall make his way back, and punish those others?" (*Odyssey* 5.23–24). In the final book he repeats these words (*Odyssey* 24.479–478).
96 Kuhns 1962, 66.

In the *Odyssey*, the conflict ends thus:

Royal son of Laertes, Odysseus, master of exploits
Hold back now! Call a halt to the great leveler, War –
don't court the rage of Zeus who rules the world!
So she commanded. He obeyed her, glad at heart.
And Athena handed down her pacts of peace
Between both sides for all the years to come (*Odyssey* 24.595–598).

In the course of the *Odyssey*, Athena devised stratagems and plans, with and without Odysseus; as the warrior goddess, she intimidates the disputants, and with Zeus' help she erases the slaying of the suitors from their families' memories. Yet the conflict is finally resolved only after Athena uses conciliatory arguments. She turns to the power of persuasion to ensure that the peace achieved is sustainable. Despite her ability to impose a coercive settlement on the parties, Athena aims at an agreed resolution, instituting a peaceful covenant and code of behavior for society in the days to come.

In the *Oresteia*, Athena establishes a court in order to resolve the dispute between Orestes and the Erinyes and break the cycle of revenge. After Orestes' acquittal, the enraged Erinyes intend to inflict a plague upon Athens, highlighting the potential disjuncture between the judicial solution and the best interests of the Athenian public. The response that Aeschylus attributes to Athena is therefore directed at the Athenians and at the Erinyes. She reminds the Erinyes of the menacing power of lightning, and the advantages to be gained by accepting the verdict:

You are not dishonored; do not with excessive wrath blight the land of mortals, goddesses that you are! I, for my part, have trust in Zeus, and – why need I speak of it? – I alone among the gods know the keys of the house wherein is sealed the lightning. But there is no need of it; let me persuade you, and do not discharge upon this land the words of an idle tongue so as to cause all things that bear fruit no more to prosper. Lull to repose the bitter force of your black wave of anger, since you shall be honored and revered and dwell with me! (*Eumenides* 824–833).

Turning to the Athenians, Athena tries to convince them of the advantages of the new dispute resolution mechanism that she intends to support from now onwards:

Such is the object of awe that you must justly dread, and so you shall have a bulwark of the land and a protector of the city such as none of human kind possesses, neither among the Scythians nor in the domains of Pelops (*Eumenides* 700–703).

In effect, Athena's mediation efforts and not the verdict is what ultimately leads to the conflict's resolution.[97] Interestingly, the section of the play devoted to the dialogue between Athena and the Erinyes after the trial is about twice as long as the description of the trial itself. As a judge, Athena fails to enforce the verdict on her own, and a full resolution of the matter is possible only by mediating a compromise that recognizes the powers behind each party.[98] The ultimate closure of the *Oresteia* then, is not a legal one: Only the goddess's rhetoric succeeds in resolving the deep-seated tensions.[99]

Athena's duality, which perhaps resonates with the profound duality at the heart of Aeschylus' drama in general, as Friedrich Nietzsche noted,[100] is also revealed in the conspicuous flaws in the judicial procedure she establishes. "The triumph of law" in the *Oresteia* is defective, as various Marxist, feminist, and other critical readings suggest.[101] Even a basic legal reading identifies several problems that characterize the judicial procedure described in the *Oresteia*, most of them relating to Athena's multiple roles.

Although in her role as the founder of the court, Athena proclaims her commitment to the Athenians' best interests and the city's prosperity, donning her judicial gown she adamantly declares her support for the defendant due to his gender, regardless of the specific matter at hand: "I vouch myself the champion of the man, not of the woman, yea, with all my soul" (*Eumenides* 737–738). She renounces her previous declaration to recuse herself from deciding in this matter and entrust it to the judges from among the Athenians, and reveals her personal bias and intention of pursuing it:

> [...] and I belong altogether to my father. Therefore I shall not give greater weight to the death of a woman, one who slew her husband, the watcher of the house; Orestes is the winner, even should the votes be equal (*Eumenides* 738–741).

Athena is often driven by emotion – sometimes rage,[102] sometimes compassion, affection and sympathy, the latter frequently being expressed toward Odysseus and his family. In the *Eumenides* her sympathy clearly lies with

---

97 On Athena as mediator, see Gagarin 1986, 42.

98 Gagarin, 1986, 66.

99 Goldhill 2004, 31.

100 See Friedrich Wilhelm Nietzsche *The Birth of Tragedy* [1872], trans. Smith Douglas (Oxford, New York: Oxford University Press, 2000), 67.

101 For details, see Goldhill 2004, 30–33.

102 For details on how Athena's anger and its appeasement drive the plots of the *Iliad* and the *Odyssey*, see Jenny Strauss-Clay, *The Wrath of Athena: Gods and Men in the Odyssey* (Princeton, NJ: Princeton University Press, 1983), 213–239 (hereinafter abbreviated as Strauss-Clay 1983).

Orestes, and the legal procedure is conducted in a manner that reinforces this sense of favoritism. Athena allows Apollo – who by his own account serves as a witness, an attorney, and the one who counseled Orestes to kill his mother – to present his arguments in Orestes' favor (*Eumenides* 574–580). After Apollo does so at some length, the Erinyes make no response and there is no discussion of the arguments in Orestes' defense. The trial ends in a tie. It is then that Athena casts her deciding vote. The Erinyes' frustration and rage is not unexpected, though they may be unfamiliar with labels that developed in later stages of the rule of law such as bias, prejudice or conflict of interests. However, when Athena realizes that the judicial outcome will not suffice, she assumes the task of appeasing the Erinyes, which is successfully accomplished.

Athena's conduct in the *Oresteia* makes it challenging to reconcile her actions with any conception of procedural justice associated with the rule of law: Orestes is her favorite, and her statements and actions clearly reflect her bias. Her derogatory remarks about women color the ancient story in blatantly patriarchal hues and charge it with gender prejudice. Athena's version of adjudication seems a manifestation of inequitableness.

The *Odyssey*, in which aggression also plays a central role, is not devoid of quasi-judicial moments. As described above, the divine pantheon serves as judicial-like panel before which Athena pleads for Odysseus. The quasi-legal procedure in the *Odyssey* is also flawed, and here, too, Athena is mainly responsible for its defects. Athena functions concurrently as counsel for the defendant Odysseus and as one of the Olympian judges of his case. At Athena's choosing, the procedure coincided with Poseidon's, who was known to be hostile toward Odysseus. Finally, after the Olympian "verdict" that allows Odysseus to return to his home, Athena also becomes the executor of the decision.

In both works, the figure of Athena constantly shifts between complementary and sometimes contradictory roles. In the *Odyssey*, in one moment she expresses the cold, ruthless logic of recompense, refering to the justice of Aegisthus' fate: "surly he goes to a death he earned in full! Let them all die so, all who do such things" (*Odyssey* 1.65–66). In another instant she is driven by emotion, speaking of the urgent need to help Odysseus: "But my heart breaks for Odysseus" (*Odyssey* 1.68). In the *Oresteia*, she is a quasi-adversarial judge, conducting the courtroom according to formal rules with the aim of deciding on Orestes' guilt for the murder of his mother: "Do you summon witnesses and proofs, sworn evidence to assist justice" (*Eumenides* 485–486), yet in another instant, her judgment seems to be based on a personal whim: "I approve the male in all things" (*Eumenides* 737). At one point she menacingly refers to her access to Zeus' dreadful thunderbolts, and in another moment she falls on her powers of persuasion and calls on the Erinyes to acknowledge "the power to charm and soothe that sits upon my tongue" (*Eumenides* 886).

In both cases, Athena's initial action – rendering "belligerent assistance" to Odysseus in the Homeric epic and establishing the court in the *Oresteia* – does not suffice to resolve the crisis of revenge. Consequently, in both works, a complementary strategy of resolution is required.

In both works, Athena is described as a mediator and conciliator, who conducts a multiparty lively, dynamic discourse that is sentsitive to the needs of all parties to the dispute, in order to arrive at a sustainable solution beneficial to society as a whole. In the context of the *Odyssey*, Athena's act of mediation and conciliation seems to acknowledge the limits of power and its inability to provide sustainable solutions to intricate conflicts. In the context of the *Oresteia*, Athena's mediation and conciliation seem to underscore the limitations of formal institutional judging. In contemporary terms, in her formal judging Athena also integrates elements of alternative dispute resolution. Thus, in restrospect, inside these classical narratives lie the seeds of the potential complexity of the judicial role; and both stories, despite the centuries and immense social transformations that separate their authors, place at the center of the narrative the figure of a goddess whose acts represent a milestone along the road to the rule of law.

Conclusion

In a study of Athens' transition to the sovereignty of law in the fifth century BC, Ostwald notes some of the milestones on this evolutionary path:

> Ephialtes' work is unthinkable without the work of Cleisthenes [...]; Cleisthenes' achievement, in its turn, was made possible only by the consequences of Solon's activity at the beginning of the sixth century; and Solon's reforms based on developments, inscrutable to us, that had followed the unification of Attica attributed by legend to Theseus [...] All were responses to historical situations that, as by-product, led to [...] the point at which the sovereignty of the people [...] could then become an ideology.[103]

In the spirit of these remarks, the rule of law became feasible only after the maturation of certain conceptions; a powerful story about the establishment of law could similarly emerge only at a certain moment of ripeness. The generative legal

---

103 Ostwald 1986, xx.

narrative could emerge and take root only at a certain moment, toward which the preceding narratives paved the path.

The constitutive moment of the judicial procedure described in the *Eumenides* is central to the conceptualization of the rule of law, and rightfully deserves the title "generative legal narrative." However, viewed against Bakhtin's "great time," it appears to be one of many landmarks along the unending efforts toward an improved legal justice, a journey that is far from its end, even today.

In the course of that journey, the *Odyssey*, an articulation that presents a potent, quasi-legal contemplation of reckoning, retribution, justice and public order, constitutes a major milestone. In the *Oresteia*, this contemplation evolves into a generative legal narrative. The space between these two great works can be likened to a slow relay race. The smoldering ember of law, its glimmer already apparent in the *Odyssey*, becomes a flaming torch when the *Oresteia*, a suitable platform in terms of timing and poetics, sets the story of the establishment of the rule of law at its center.

The man whose fate would light the torch of law would not be opportunistic and cunning Odysseus, who unhesitatingly killed dozens of suitors and handmaidens to ensure his successful reinstatement, but rather the tormented, anguished Orestes, who lost his sister and his father and murdered his mother and her lover. Each of them is led toward a different end by Athena, the goddess of war and wisdom and the great patron of civil political life. In the *Odyssey* Athena was concerned with the public interest; she leads the adversaries to a consensual agreement, "[...] handed down her pacts of peace between both sides for all the years to come" (*Odyssey* 24.595 – 598). In the *Oresteia*, she also considers it her duty to act "in good will toward my citizens" (*Eumenides* 927).

The generative legal narrative fully emerges in the Oresteia to present a model of action that mainly aligns with the interests of the privileged patriarchal elite. The *Odyssey* relates the exploits of an elite that bears limited responsibility for its actions and choices, and in that respect, the formal rule of law depicted in the *Oresteia* will change little. Orestes, a member of the privileged elite, is ultimately extricated from legal payment for the murder he committed. The elite's privileged status will continue to extend to the new institution of law. Nonetheless the constitutive moment described in the *Eumenides* is of immense importance. Once it was presented, albeit in the imperfect form advocated by Athena, society could no longer do without it.

Both of these great works, the *Odyssey* and the *Oresteia*, reflect the meaning of the paradigm *of law alongside literature*, which exposes the structural failures in law together with the unending aspiration to improve it.[104] Both are meaningful stations on law's long and winding road.

104 For elaboration on the paradigm of *law alongside literature*, see Almog 2007, 756–761.

Chapter 3
From The Iliad to the Odyssey – Toward the Juridification of Anger

Perhaps the great lawmaker [...]
Is the legitimate heir to Homeric wisdom.
Rachel Bespaloff, Priam and Achilles Break Bread

Law Making and Homeric Wisdom

Aristotle famously précises the *Odyssey* as follows:

> A certain man is absent from home for many years; he is jealously watched by Poseidon, and left desolate. Meanwhile his home is in a wretched plight– suitors are wasting his substance and plotting against his son. At length, tempest-tost, he himself arrives; he makes certain persons acquainted with him; he attacks the suitors with his own hand, and is himself preserved while he destroys them.[105]

All the rest is merely episodes. But the episodes, as Aristotle himself notes, are paramount. They extend across time and space. They move between the present and events that took place in the past. Some of them present a somewhat realistic picture, while others transport us to spaces such as Mt. Olympus, the home of the gods, or Hades, the world of the dead. The result is a diverse, vibrant narrative that deals with family and communal life, journeys on land and at sea, and economic, public, and artistic endeavors. In addition, the *Odyssey* captivates us with stories of complex relationships and of the adventures and emotional lives of royal protagonists, warriors, serving men and women, and gods and goddesses.

Formally, the scope of the *Iliad* is much narrower. The narrative it lays out covers a brief, delimited period of time: fourteen days and nights, including four days of combat. The events transpire in two locations: inside the besieged city of Troy, intent on its battle for survival, and the Greek camp outside the city, determined to destroy it. Despite this narrow frame, the *Iliad* is a wonderfully complex text that deals with a wealth of topics including love, jealousy, friendship, devotion, and sacrifice among gods and goddesses, men and women. Yet at its core, the epic is a story of deadly war.

---

105 *The Poetics of Aristotle*, Butcher trans., 111.

https://doi.org/10.1515/9783110766110-005

Despite this fundamental difference between the *Odyssey* and the *Iliad*, the works are essentially similar. Both describe a society characterized by the same social values and rules. Both tell about myths that are related to the Heroic Age identified with the Mycenaean period, an age that ended many generations before the time of telling.[106] Conceptions of the rule of law, or of an all-embracing law to which society is subject, are alien to this age. The heroes whose lives stand at the center of the Homeric epic are men of the upper classes, whose lives are focused on excellence in battle, personal victories, and aspirations for fame. The typical Homeric hero is preoccupied with pursuits of glory and defending honor, and is committed to little else, certainly not to the dictates of justice.

Does the society described in the epics reflect the social values and rules of the Heroic Age, or of a period several centuries later? In his famous book *The World of Odysseus*, classical historian Moses Finley asserts that besides reflecting ancient myths, the Homeric text appears to reflect rather faithfully the society that existed at the time it was composed, circa the eighth century BC, as well as its social values and norms. Discernible in this post-Mycenaean society are the initial buds of law, on which the epic sheds light.

The first intimations of law – direct and indirect references to law and to social life subject to law – with which the Homeric epics are saturated were described earlier. One important intimation appears in Book XVIII of the *Iliad*, entitled "The Shield of Achilles." The reader may recall that Hephaestus, master craftsman of the gods, made use of all "his craft and cunning" (*Iliad* 18.563) to create the images engraved upon the shield he prepared for Achilles. One image shows a judge or mediator who peacefully resolves a dispute between two men in the matter of compensation for a murder, apparently according to contemporary practice (*Iliad* 18.580 – 592). It follows that judicial or quasi-judicial procedure was not alien to the world of the *Iliad*, and strict and clear social rules regulated the procedure of revenge in the society the epic describes.

Moreover, the epic generally depicts a sophisticated social order, in which economics, politics, war, and family life and social life are conducted in accordance with known norms and rules. As Peter Rose notes, the *Iliad* paints "a picture of social, political and economic relationships familiar to the poet and his audience."[107]

---

106 On the dating of the epic and the Heroic Age that preceded it, see Finley 1972, Chapter 2.
107 Peter W. Rose, *"Class Ambivalence in the "Odyssey," Historia: Zeitschrift für Alte Geschichte* 24.2 (1975): 129 – 149, 131 – 132.

The Homeric heroes do not come across as free spirits who accept or reject social rules and strictures on a whim or as they choose. Quite the opposite: all the epic heroes are responsive to social authority, demonstrating some or other degree of subservience to the social order and a known value system. As James Redfield aptly states:

> Homeric actors are seen as embedded in a social fabric; they are persons whose acts and consciousness are the enactment of social forces which play upon them.[108]

The social structures of the Homeric communities function by means of a discourse that is conducted in the public sphere. Such assemblies, which echo ideas of deliberation and what could be ascribed today to the field of public law, served as the primary means for regulating the interactions between the community's members and its leaders, making it possible to conduct a well-ordered social life. The *Odyssey* tells of assemblies held in Ithaca, in the city of the Phaeacians, and in other sites, while the *Iliad* refers to assemblies held both in besieged Troy and in the Greek camp. In both the *Iliad* and the *Odyssey*, public discourse in a designated location is one of the hallmarks of a community.[109] Even in the absence of written laws, the assemblies provide a certain manifestation of the principle of fairness and create structured opportunities for argumentation and persuasion.[110]

The meaning of a literary work is fluid and dynamic, with the text changing its form upon every encounter with a reader and the reader's own time. At the same time, the examination of the literary reveals changing conceptions of justice and morality and their relation to the rule of law.[111] From this multilayered point of departure, I examine the relationships between the Homeric epics and the evolution of law and the way in which the epics reflect the contemporary notions of law.

As I propose, a gradual striving toward the rule of law emerges from both works, not only in those early allusions to law that appear in both, but also,

---

108 James M. Redfield, *Nature and Culture in the Iliad: The Tragedy of Hector* (Durham: Duke University Press, 1994), 20 (hereinafter abbreviated as: Redfield 1994).

109 Karl J. Hölkeskamp, "Arbitrators, Lawgivers and the 'Codification of Law' in Archaic Greece: Problems and Perspectives," *Metis. Anthropologie des mondes anciens* 7 (1992): 49–81, 64 (hereinafter abbreviated as: Hölkeskamp,1992)

110 Hölkeskamp 1992, 61: "[f]airly specific notions of what was 'just' ... were indeed at the very heart of the earliest, 'Homeric' Greek communities."

111 In this regard, see Arthur W. H. Adkins, *Merit and Responsibility: A Study in Greek Values* (Oxford: Clarendon Press, 1960), 51 (hereinafter abbreviated as: Adkins, 1960); Michael Gagarin 1987, "Morality in Homer," *Classical Philology* 82.4 (1987): 285–306.

and perhaps especially, from the absence of law, and specifically the appalling price that its absence exacts, which both the *Iliad* and the *Odyssey* highlight.

My interest here is not in an anthropological, historical, or jurisprudential discussion of questions such as "What is law?" or "What the relation is between law and justice?"[112] Nor do I address the question regarding which social order and worldview are reflected in the epics – those of the Mycenaean period of its narrative or those extant at the time it was written.[113] My interest lies in observing, through the spyhole provided by these great literary works, the gradual movement of human society toward law, a movement that the epics grippingly implay.

According to the exploration proposed here, the law does not exist a priori. It does not "act" in a particular way or "avoid" acting in a different way. Law is not an essence personified, capable of independent movement. In my view, law is an interpretative notion shaped by circles of discourse and a dynamic and constantly developing framework of thinking. This discourse is studded with trends, interpretations, fashions, and discoveries. It is an ever evolving tapestry, in which the Homeric epic has woven threads that are discernible to this day.

Suggestions to draw a link between the epics and conceptions of law and justice are not new. A venerable humanistic tradition celebrates the ancient Greek poets, Homer first and foremost, as the midwives of a later civilization based on foundations of law and morality. This tradition sees the Greek myths, which served as the building blocks of ancient Greek poetry, as a collection of narratives capable of guiding individuals and societies in any age toward an optimal political and social existence. The poets of ancient Greece, writes George Puttenham in this spirit, were "the first lawmakers to the people."[114] The Homeric text promotes an idea of social life dependent upon law and order, and provides a key to understanding legal order as a prerequisite of a tolerable social existence. The epics contain frequent intimations of law, which serve to support this position.

There are, however, other approaches that see the ancient myths and their reflection in the Homeric epics as a representation of destructive collective vio-

---

112 For the leading sources dealing with these matters, see Cantarella 2001, 473–475.

113 To reiterate, the epic was written long before the development of the *polis* and its customary law. The prevailing view is that the Homeric epic predates by at least a century the first written law in Western civilization, which prohibited personal revenge and was promulgated in 620 BC by Dracon (Cantarella 2001, 474). Nonetheless, written laws seem to have existed already in the mid-seventh century BC, predating the epic (Gagarin 1986 19).

114 George Puttenham, *The Art of English Poesy*, eds. Frank Whigham and Wayne A. Rebhorn (Ithaca, NY; London: Cornell University Press, 2007), 97.

lence, and an expression of ingrained violent impulses with which humanity is cursed. Such approaches read the myths and the Homeric epics as cautionary tales of unbridled aggression, accounts of a moral rift, echoing the monstrosity of innocents murdered without accountability.[115] According to such views, "myth and violence have been inseparable."[116]

A critical distinction is commonly made between the treatment of matters of morality and justice in the *Iliad* and the *Odyssey*.[117] According to one reading, in the *Iliad* personal will and interest reign supreme, whereas in the *Odyssey* the personal element joins the demands of justice, even if the representation of justice is yet embryonic.[118] Jasper Griffin hones the distinction between the works. The *Odyssey*, he states, is far from the grim conception of the absence of justice with which the *Iliad* concludes. From the outset, Zeus of the *Odyssey* accepts the challenge to manifest justice through the award of just deserts for human actions. Ultimately, the sinners are punished, and Odysseus' victory is presented as one reflecting a theory of justice.[119]

An even more adamant view of the matter is taken by Martin West, whose comprehensive research is devoted to identifying essential differences between the *Iliad* and the *Odyssey*.[120] According to West, one of the major differences (besides the different narrative tools and poetic choices in the two works) stems from the fact that the author of the *Odyssey* is guided by the distinction between good and evil. He lives in a society which, despite the absence of a written legal codex, is governed by norms of fairness and propriety. Accordingly, in the *Odyssey* the gods are presented as an almost united body intent on doing good, supporting and rewarding worthy individuals, and punishing those whose actions demand retribution. By contrast, the author of the *Iliad* depicts the gods and goddesses as acting in their own interest, or on personal whims and arbitrarily. The fate of human beings in the *Iliad* is not the result of divine efforts to determine whether their actions were good or bad, but is instead based on whether the humans pleased or failed to please a certain god or goddess. These differen-

---

115 For such approaches, see Anna-Maria Hartmann, "An Undemocratic Turn?" *The Cambridge Quarterly* 47.3 (2018): 272–273 (hereinafter abbreviated as: Hartmann 2018).
116 Hartmann 2018, 272.
117 For a discussion of these differences, see Guthrie 1955, 117; Hugh Lloyd-Jones, *The Justice of Zeus* (Berkeley: University of California Press, 1983), 27.
118 Finley 1972, 37.
119 Griffin 2004, 47.
120 See Martin Litchfield West, *The Making of the Odyssey* (Oxford; New York: Oxford University Press, 2014) (hereinafter abbreviated as: West 2014).

ces are so essential, in West's view, that they can be reconciled only by concluding that the *Iliad* and the *Odyssey* were written by different authors.[121]

This chapter does not aim to decide between these positions, or even to identify similarities and differences in themes or ideas associated with law or justice in the *Odyssey* and the *Iliad*. My point of departure is that such themes exist in both texts. Neither work assumes a space devoid of norms; both of them exhibit, in certain contexts, an essentialist preoccupation with the role of justice in constituting social life.[122] In both the *Odyssey* and the *Iliad*, Homeric society is still far removed from the future that holds within it the emergence of the illustrious *polis*, one of whose fundaments would be written and institutionalized law. But already evident in this society is a prelude to the institution that would later be identified as "law."[123] In this chapter I track the intricate nature of this movement in each of the two works. To that end I turn the spotlight on a specific component of the Homeric epics – the way in which these works develop the consequences associated with anger.

A prominent term in the classical Greek heritage is *mēnis*, usually translated as anger or wrath.[124] Anger is also a key concept that has always been associated with law. At the foundation of law lies the regimentation of anger. The subordination of anger and the impulse to act out of anger constitutes a core foundation of the rule of law. The *Oresteia* is a generative legal story that describes a dramatic moment in this context, when both gods and human mortals renounce the choice that had been taken for granted in the ancient myth – the choice to kill because of anger. The Homeric epics are almost a necessary prequel. They put forward a powerful representation of the toll society pays for allowing unbridled, rampant fury, thus presenting an antithesis of the concept of legal order, and promoting the idea that legal order is essential for well-ordered human existence.

This chapter looks at the occurrences of wrath in the *Iliad* and the *Odyssey*. The first part of the chapter focuses on the wrath of Odysseus and of Achilles, and the second part concerns the wrath of gods and goddesses. The third and final part describes how, through the prism of the poetic treatment of wrath,

---

121 West 2014, 48.

122 On this matter, see Luban 1997, 298.

123 See Hölkeskamp 1992, 51.

124 See Jenny Strauss-Clay, "The Anger of Achilles: 'Mēnis' in Greek Epic (Book Review)," *The American Journal of Philology* 118.4 (1997): 631–634, 631–634. For a broad overview of the conceptual world relating to anger in Greek classical culture, see Leonard Charles Muellner, *The Anger of Achilles: 'Menis' in Greek Epic* (Ithaca, NY: Cornell University Press, 1996).

both works promote the generative story of the rule of law that would appear several generations later in tragedy.

Achilles: "giving in to his power, his brute force and wild pride"

The Trojan War advances upon waves of wrath of increasing intensity. Although the *Iliad* also tells of the terrible wrath of gods and goddesses, at the center of this work is fury ascribed to a mortal. The narrative is organized around Achilles' rage which is introduced as a generative element already in its first lines:

> Rage-Goddess, sing the rage of Peleus' son Achilles,
> murderous, doomed, that cost the Achaeans countless losses (*Iliad* 1.1–2).

Moreover, Achilles comes across as being serially wrathful. The *Iliad* describes three waves of increasingly intense fury, each culminating in progressively disastrous consequences.

The first wave of rage is sparked by a dispute over the division of the spoils of war. In the tenth year of the war, Agamemnon, leader of the Greek army, takes for himself the maiden Chryseis, daughter of a priest of Apollo, as a prize of war to which he is entitled. Agamemnon refuses her father's request to ransom his daughter, and in retaliation Apollo strikes the Greek army with a plague. When a prophecy confronts Agamemnon with the connection between the large number of victims of the plague and his refusal to heed the priest's request, Agamemnon relents and relinquishes Chryseis. But in her stead he demands to be given Briseis, another captive whom Achilles has already claimed as his own prize of victory. Achilles feels that the demand is an affront to his honor. Enraged, as he ponders whether to kill Agamemnon or restrain himself and curb his anger, Athena appears to him and instructs him to suffice with verbal abuse.

Achilles obeys. He gives up Briseis, lashes out at Agamemnon, who is not loath to return fire (*Iliad* 1.263). Their dispute remains charged and unresolved. In his anger, Achilles abandons preparations for the battle against the Trojans and remains in his camp. He calls on his mother, the immortal nymph Thetis, beseeching her to aid Troy in the battle and defeat his erstwhile comrades in arms. Thetis, deeply affected by her son's suffering, assents. She advises him to "rage on at the Achaeans, just keep clear of every foray in the fighting" (*Iliad* 1.504). While Achilles follows her counsel and continues to fume in camp, his mother extracts a promise from Zeus to help the Trojans in the fighting. The Greeks suffer a series of successive defeats, with the Trojans almost reaching the Greek ships.

The first wave of wrath culminates, then, in an active effort by Achilles to thwart the Greeks' battle plans. After he succeeds in doing so, his wrath subsides somewhat, but does not dissolve. Due to the grim situation on the battlefield, several Greek leaders are sent to appease Achilles and to persuade him to return to fight at their side. They report that Agamemnon has offered to return Briseis to him, to wed his daughter to him, and to bestow many gifts upon him. Since Achilles' wrath has subsided but not ceased, he still refuses to join the battle himself, yet he agrees to send his good friend Patroclus into the fray, clad in Achilles' own armor. In the ensuing battle, the Trojan hero Hector kills Patroclus.

It is the death of his beloved friend that ignites the second wave of wrath in Achilles. He and Agamemnon are reconciled, and he accepts the latter's gifts. Since the armor he gave Patroclus is lost, he uses new weapons made for him by the Olympian metalsmith Hephaestus. Achilles again finds himself "bursting with rage" (*Iliad* 22.369). This wave of fury comes to a climax in a mass slaughter of the Trojans by Achilles, filling the river Skamandros with bodies and coloring it red. Achilles eventually catches up with Hector, overcomes and kills him too.

But the killing of many Trojans, including his main adversary, does nothing to calm the storm in Achilles' soul, and in fact arouses a third wave of wrath, which culminates in his abuse of Hector's body over the course of eleven days. In the wake of this exceptional offense, Apollo protests to Zeus against Achilles who "outrages the senseless clay in all his fury" (*Iliad* 24.65). On the twelfth day, the gods contrive a meeting between King Priam, Hector's grieving father, and Achilles. Priam's entreaties finally succeed in extinguishing the flames of Achilles' fury. At dawn, after spending the night as a guest of the man who slew his son, Priam returns to Troy with his son's body. The *Iliad* concludes with the story of Hector's burial.

Despite this concluding scene wherein conciliated Achilles relinquishes Hector's body, he remains a protagonist whose main attribute is anger. Anger is Achilles' engine, which turns into the driver of the *Iliad*. It is anger that has fascinated many and inspired interpretations at times diametrically opposed. According to several views, Achilles' wrath speaks to a striving toward justice, autonomy, and rule of law. I begin with these.

According to Luban's reading, by curbing the anger aroused by Agamemnon's demand for Briseis, Achilles moves from a society in which affront to one's honor is the cardinal offense toward a social existence centered on a striving for justice. Achilles cannot express in words or give a name to this vague expectation, which is in effect an expectation of justice.[125] Nonetheless, it is potently present and is reflected in his choice to withdraw from the fighting:

> Achilles proceeds along a trajectory that leads him out of the honor-and-compromise culture of Book I and into a moral universe with very different concerns [...] which [...] are closely related to what *we* call justice.[126]

On this reading, this is a moment of revelation, a moment in which Achilles becomes conscious of the phenomenon of injustice. His surrender of Briseis is a manifestation of injustice, and his refusal to accept the compromises that Agamemnon and many others offer is in the nature of a "quest for justice."[127] According to Luban, it is not Achilles' willingness to die in battle but his willingness to sacrifice his life in pursuit of justice that makes him a heroic character.[128] A similar reading sees the character of Achilles as the moral kernel of the *Iliad* that marks the transition from a shame culture to a guilt culture.[129] Another interpretation along such lines is suggested by Peter Ahrensdorf, who believes that Achilles is endowed with a rare moral quality, underscored by the scene of his reconciliation with Priam, which highlights Achilles' moral magnanimity. This scene stands out particularly in contrast to Odysseus, whose final action in the *Odyssey* stems from his inability to loosen the grip rage has on him. Achilles, on this view, demonstrates an ability to act out of compassion, making him the best of the Achaeans.[130]

Such a conception draws a link between Achilles' character and the general human aspiration to strive for justice. From this perspective, despite Achilles' inability to express his arguments and expectations using the existing vocabulary, the *Iliad* marks the sunset of the heroic order and a transition toward a new social and moral existence. The pursuit of justice connects Achilles' wrath to the

---

125 Adam Parry, "The Language of Achilles," *Transactions and Proceedings of the American Philological Association* 87 (1956): 1–7. In this well-known article, Adam Parry describes the dearth of a conceptual vocabulary which characterizes the figure of Achilles, and the tragic price of this shortfall: "Achilles has no language with which to express his disillusionment. Yet he expresses it. He asks questions that cannot be answered and makes demands that cannot be met."
126 David Luban, "Some Greek Trials: Order and Justice in Homer, Hesiod, Aeschylus and Plato," *Tennessee Law Review* 54.2 (1986): 297–311, 285 (hereinafter abbreviated as: Luban 1986).
127 Luban 1986, 290.
128 Luban 1986, 291.
129 James A. Arieti, "Achilles' Guilt," *The Classical Journal* 80.3 (1985): 193–203, 194 (hereinafter abbreviated as Arieti 1985).
130 Peter J. Ahrensdorf, *Homer on the Gods and Human Virtue: Creating the Foundations of Classical Civilization* (New York: Cambridge University Press 2014, 23. In this context, also see Redfield 1994, 219.

dissolution of an obsolete world-picture and its replacement by a new order, to be founded upon written laws. One of the hallmarks of the new order is the decline of the heroic code, which is maintained by shared rituals such as meals, sacrifices, and gift-giving (which Achilles also rejects as bereft of sufficient meaning), and its replacement by a more advanced code of conduct, to be instituted in the *polis*. In the *polis*, written laws will apply, to better govern the relationships and commitments of all members of society.[131] On this view, at the core of Achilles' motivations lies – hidden perhaps from even his own consciousness – a fervent yearning for what is today perceived as justice. Wrath is the means that enables Achilles to renounce the heroic code of conduct and strive toward a better social order.

The very same character has also elicited a diametrically opposite interpretation that underscores Achilles' unbounded selfishness and cruelty.[132] On such a view, his character represents one of the most striking and problematic aspects of the declining heroic culture – the constant pursuit of honor, and the heavy price paid by society for what was understood as an affront to personal honor. This hero, however, clearly has the linguistic abilities to express a longing for a new and more just world of values, as evident from Achilles' detailed description of his feelings. In effect, Achilles is far from beeing speechless regarding the way he grasps the injury to him. Achilles' elaborate and well-argued remarks in this context do not sound like a hesitant striving of an individual toward an abstract idea of justice and lacks the appropriate language and concepts. Instead, Achilles offers an accurate and succinct description of the situation: "the man disgraces me" (*Iliad* 1.420). To this, Achilles affixes a stream of verbosity that details the scope of the affront to his honor, the intensity of the injury he is experiencing, and what he experiences as Agamemnon's betrayal.

It is interesting that Homer chooses to tell us that Achilles' rage does not stem from any special importance that Briseis holds for him, or because he loves her or has developed a fondness for her. Several days after the intolerable insult and the first wave of wrath, when Achilles decides to reconcile with Agamemnon after Patroclus' death, Achilles bemoans the fact that Briseis was not killed in the battle, for then he and Agamemnon might have been spared their quarrel:

---

131 Steve Nimis, "The Language of Achilles: Construction vs. Representation," *The Classical World* 79 (1986): 217–225, 223.

132 For such a view on Achilles, see Deborah De Chiara-Quenzer, "Aristotle, Achilles, Courage, and Moral Failure," in *Looking at Beauty to Kalon in Western Greece: Selected Essays from the 2018 Symposium on the Heritage of Western Greece*, eds. Heather L. Reid and Tony Leyh (Sioux City, IA: Parnassos Press, 2019), 189–202.

Agamemnon-was it better for both of us, after all,
for you and me to rage at each other, raked by anguish,
consumed by heartsick strife, all for a young girl?
If only Artemis had cut her down at the ships–
with one quick shaft
that day I destroyed Lyrnessus, chose her as my prize. (*Iliad* 19.63 – 68)

To the contemporary reader it is obvious that the conveyance of Briseis and Chryseis as objects from one man's possession into another's to serve as sex slaves is much more offensive and deplorable than the insult to Achilles' honor and arouses his wrath. From such a viewpoint, the lack of voice Homer assigns these women is also disturbing and especially striking in contrast to the detailed bickering of the furious men.

However, my interest here is to examine Achilles' wrath from our best understanding of the perspective of the time of the story, in order to ascertain the role that the literary representation of anger plays in the journey toward the establishment of law. From such a perspective, in light of the norms extant in heroic society, it is doubtful that Achilles' first wave of wrath is justified. Finley explains that female captives were distributed among the victors as marks of honor, and the more meritorious soldiers who deserved a significant mark of honor received the youngest and most beautiful captive.[133] According to this norm of "quantitative honor,"[134] Chryseis was apparently the first prize, the most significant mark of honor, to which Agamemnon was entitled by dint of his standing. Agamemnon indeed asserts that he is interested in Chryseis due to her "quality": "Indeed, I prefer her by far, the girl herself. I want her mine in my own house! I rank her higher than Clytemnestra, my wedded wife" (*Iliad* 1.131–134).

When Agamemnon is forced to relinquish his prize of war in the interests of the collective, he is entitled under the prevailing norm to receive the second prize, the next mark of honor in line. The way the story is delivered indicates that Agamemnon acted by right as head of the Greek armies and in keeping with custom when he demanded that Briseis be given to him by Achilles.[135]

Confirmation of this is provided by Nestor's conciliatory remarks in the course of the assembly devoted to efforts to resolve the dispute. Although Nestor (unsuccessfully) tries to persuade Agamemnon to retract his demand for Briseis because she was already awarded to Achilles, he nonetheless reminds Achilles

---

133 See Finley 1972, 140.
134 Arieti 1985, 193.
135 See Adkins 1960, 51.

that it is fair and right to accede to Agamemnon's demands: "no one can match the honors dealt a king, you know" (*Iliad* 1.326).

Achilles, however, is neither willing to subject himself to this principle nor to recognize the authority of a more senior commander. Agamemnon accurately characterizes Achilles as someone who "wants to rule over all, to lord it over all, give out orders to every man in sight" (*Iliad* 1.337–338).

The first wave of wrath prompts Achilles to not only hurl insults at the commander of the army and refrain from participating in the fighting, but to effectively act in traitorous fashion. To exact his revenge on Agamemnon, he implores his mother to persuade Zeus to support the Trojans against the Greeks:

> persuade him, somehow, to help the Trojan cause,
> to pin the Achaeans back against their ships,
> trap them round the bay and mow them down.
> So all can reap the benefits of their king
> so even mighty Atrides can see how mad he was
> to disgrace Achilles, the best of the Achaeans! (*Iliad* 1.485–490)

Achilles, then, is so focused on the insult he suffered that it overshadows any other obligation or commitment he might have made. By contrast, Agamemnon is willing to accommodate the affront to his honor caused by the insults Achilles hurled at him, even to offer far-reaching conciliatory gestures, and to forgo his right to Briseis despite his fervent desire to keep her. Agamemnon acts like a leader who demonstrates responsibility for the fate of the entire army and for the outcome of the mission entrusted to him. Achilles, on the other hand, dispenses with duty or responsibility, and his actions seem to stem solely from personal motivations.

Looking at the dispute between the two against the background of other contexts in which myth refers to the figure of Agamemnon further underscores the huge difference between Agamemnon and Achilles. When the Greek fleet gathered at Aulis to set sail to fight Troy, the myth tells us[136] that the winds stalled and prevented them from embarking. According to the seer Calchas, the incident was caused by the anger of Artemis: The goddess would only be appeased if Agamemnon, the leader of the armies, sacrificed his daughter Iphigenia. Agamemnon instructs his wife to send Iphigenia to Aulis on the false pretext that he intends to give her to Achilles in marriage. When she arrives, he places her upon

---

136 The best known retelling of this myth is Euripides, *Iphigenia in Aulis*, trans. by Nicholas Rudall (Chicago: Ivan R. Dee, 1997).

the altar and kills her. Appeased, Artemis releases the winds and the fleet can set out on its way.

The sacrifice of Agamemnon's daughter so the fleet can set sail is, of course, a moral outrage. However, Achilles' sacrifice of many Greek warriors, driven (even partially) by a desire to vent his own anger, is no less, and perhaps even more of a moral outrage. In his defense, Agamemnon might have argued (even if we vehemently reject it, as did his wife Clytemnestra) that sacrificing his daughter was a terrible personal price that he chose to pay, as leader, for the benefit of all. The only argument that Achilles can raise in his defense is that he acted out of anger and indignation. On one side, then, we have Agamemnon, whom the ancient myths depict as a man who shows an absolute and unlimited commitment to the collective Greek interest, and sacrifices his daughter in the name of his commitment. The myth tells us also that Agamemnon paid with his life for this decision. Iphigenia's sacrifice was a major consideration in Clytemnestra's decision to murder her husband upon his return from Troy. "By the justice of my child, by ruin, by revenge [...] On the blood of my house I sacrificed the man." These are the words that Aeschylus puts in Clytemnestra's mouth in the play *Agamemnon*, which describes the murder.[137] Agamemnon's commitment to his soldiers and his mission is also evident in the description of the battles depicted in the *Iliad*. Agamemnon diligently prepares for the clashes with the Trojans and demonstrates great personal bravery (as described in exceptional detail in Book XI). On the other side stands Achilles, whose commitment to the common interest is so weak that, because of the outrage to the quality of his plunder, he chooses to engage in what today would be conceptualized as the crime of treason, one of the gravest in any criminal corpus.

In a similar direction, Bernard Knox draws a comparison between Achilles and Hector. In his view, Hector represents worthy cultural values, including a willingness to protect the city and the community, even at a heavy personal price. In contrast, Achilles "[i]n a private quarrel has caused the death of many of his own fellow soldiers, who now in a private quarrel thinks only on revenge [...]"[138]

Achilles' second wave of anger is set in motion by the death of Patroclus. Achilles decides to send his friend into battle in his stead, and prays to Zeus to return Patroclus home safely. Zeus, however, refuses. Patroclus, who disre-

---

137 *An Oresteia: Agamemnon by Aeschylus; Elektra by Sophocles; Orestes by Euripides*, trans. by Anne Carson, 2009, p. 65; 1432.

138 Knox's remarks appear in the introduction to Fagles' translation of the Odyssey. See Bernard Knox, "Introduction to The Iliad," in *The Iliad*, trans. Robert Fagles (London: The Folio Society, 1996), liii (hereinafter abbreviated as Knox 1996).

gards Achilles' warning not to confront Hector, is killed by Hector. The first wave of Achilles' wrath, then, leads directly to the deaths of many Greeks and also the death of his best friend.

But Achilles does not blame himself; he does not consider himself responsible for his friend's death. He is not angry at Zeus who disregarded his pleas on behalf of his friend, nor is he angry at Patroclus who failed to heed his warning. He is angry at Agamemnon, "just like the anger Agamemnon king of men has roused within me now" (*Iliad* 18.130–131), and is most angry at Hector, even though the latter did nothing "unjust" by killing Patroclus in battle. The Trojans, with Hector at their head, were conducting a life or death struggle against an enemy that had come to destroy them, as expected of them as warriors defending their city. Patroclus and Hector were both consciously risking their lives on the battlefield, and their conduct complies with the warrior norms of the Homeric epic.[139] Even if Achilles' sorrow and grief at the death of his friend is understandable, the second wave of wrath he succumbs to, which is directed at Hector, reflects a desire to extract vengeance and has nothing to do with justice.

When Achilles decides to return to the battlefield to avenge his friend's death, Odysseus and Agamemnon try to convince him to agree to allow the warriors some necessary rest and sustenance before going out to battle the Trojans. Achilles replies, "I have no taste for food – what I really crave is slaughter and blood and the choking groans of men" (*Iliad* 19.255–256). Again, Achilles' behavior is self-centered and irrational, his anger holding higher place than the needs and interests of the other warriors. When he reaches the battlefield, he rampages, driven wild not by a desire to achieve Greek victory but only by personal vengeance. Such an impulse to kill stands in contradiction to any form of moral consciousness.[140]

Achilles' third wave of wrath targeted on Hector's body. Even if the abuse of enemy corpses was acceptable in the heroic code and by the custom of the times, Achilles' actions – dragging the body around the camp behind a chariot three times a day, for eleven consecutive days – and his intention to throw Hector's body to the dogs go far beyond what was seen as proportional by the standards of the era, so much so that divine intervention was urgently required.[141] Apollo denounces Achilles before the gods – "That man without a shred of decency in

---

139 See Griffin 1980, 14.

140 As Nancy Worman states, "What kind of moral judge could such an alienated and furious warrior possibly be?" See Nancy Worman, "Reflection: Achilles and Homer's Iliad," in *Moral Motivation: A History*, ed. Iakovos Vasiliou (New York, NY: Oxford University Press, 2016), 39–43.

141 For details, see Samuel Elliot Basset, "Achilles' Treatment of Hector's Body," *Transaction and Proceeding of the American Philological Association* 64 (1933): 41–65, 64.

his heart" (*Iliad* 24.47) – and speaks of the outrage that his actions arouse among the gods and goddesses. Zeus is persuaded and dictates a settlement: Achilles will return the body in return for a ransom paid by Hector's father. Achilles' mother Thetis is sent to persuade her son to submit to Zeus' edict. Only then does Achilles agree that "The man who brings the ransom can take away the body" (*Iliad* 24.169). King Priam, Hector's bereaved father, appears before Achilles, kisses his hands, offers him the ransom gifts, and launches into a long entreaty for the release of the body. Achilles acquiesces to the bereaved father's request, but holds him back overnight to attend a festive meal before allowing him to set out on his way with Hector's body.

Is Homer relating a noble act of exalted humanity? Does Achilles really demonstrate "tremendous compassion and understanding for Priam and for all the Trojans"?[142] Does his encounter with Priam, as Redfield suggests, create a rare enclave in which two enemies, sequestered from their communities and protected by the gods, mourn together and discover their deeply shared humanity?[143] And most importantly for our matter here, is Homer telling us about a reconciliation which leads, as Paul Mazon suggests, to "the death of the wrath"[144] ("la mort de la colère") and an appropriate closure of the issue of wrath both for Achilles and for the circles of people surrounding him?[145]

It is difficult for me to read Book XXIV of the *Iliad* this way. Taking into consideration what Homer tells, I find it hard to imagine that Priam – who kneels before the man who has killed his son and kisses his hands, and declares "I have endured what no one on earth has ever done before" (*Iliad* 24.590) – undergoes anything less than excruciating torture during the hours he is forced to spend in Achilles' company until the release of his son's body. After Achilles announces that he is prepared to return the body, Priam begs not to tarry, not even to sit down, "not while Hector lies uncared-for in your camp!" (*Iliad* 24.649), but Achilles, who is used to getting his way, threatens Priam with the terrible consequences of his anger. Achilles continues to behave in character: He admonishes Priam, reminds him of his terrible power, and the fact that no one can oppose his will, and threatens to kill him despite Zeus' edict:

---

142 As suggested by Ahrensdorf 2014, 255.
143 For Redfield's description of the encounter, see Redfield 1994.
144 Paul Mazon, Paul Chantraine, Pierre Collart and Rene Langumier, *Introduction à l'Iliade* (Paris: Belles Lettres, 1943), 230. I thank Prof. Margalit Finkelberg for this reference and for help regarding this point.
145 For a position in this spirit, according to which Achilles and Priam's encounter resolves the issue of wrath from the psychological, philosophical and artistic aspects, see Margalit Finkelberg, *Homer* (Tel Aviv: The Haim Rubin Tel Aviv University Press, 2014) (Hebrew), 122.

So don't anger me now. Don't stir my raging heart still more.
Or under my own roof I may not spare your life, old man
suppliant that you are – may break the laws of Zeus! (*Iliad* 24.667–669)

Priam is forced to dine and stay the night with Achilles. He does it for fear of his life: "The old man was terrified. He obeyed the order" (*Iliad* 24.670). Not only is this far from a demonstration of compassion or empathy, forcing the aged father to remain in the company of his son's killer and the desecrator of the body can be seen as another example of the abuse that Achilles inflicts on others. Even if we attempt to cast Achilles' behavior in a more sympathetic light, and to view his encounter with Priam as a period of time that served his emotional needs and enabled him to overcome his grief at his friend's death, neither the return of the body (which is forced upon Achilles by the divine edict and his mother's wishes) nor coercing Priam into being a guest provides a satisfactory solution or closure to the theme of raging fury, which lies at the heart of the *Iliad*. Achilles' abuse of Hector's body, which was appalling even by the standards of his time, ended only as a result of massive divine intervention involving several gods and his mother's participation. Ultimately, the entire episode – the abuse of Hector's body and its release to Priam – underscores the terrifying aspect of Achilles' character, and the role of vengeance as an ongoing threat to human society.

Each wave of Achilles' wrath distances society further from conceptions of justice or morality. His character is an amalgam of warning signs against situations in which anger unchecked has fatal and far-reaching consequences that are detrimental to society as a whole. Such a character highlights the need for societal instruments that can contain wrath and protect society against it. Such tools, as the future shows, can only be provided by law. The tale of the failure of the delegation sent to appease Achilles (in Book IX of the *Iliad*) clearly demonstrates the shortcomings of all pre-legal tools.

Phoenix, who is a sort of father to Achilles, tells him that his anger ignites a spirit of destruction that will rebound against the entire army (*Iliad* 9.601). There is nothing wrong with wrath in itself, Phoenix points out, but when Achilles receives offers of gifts and remonstrations to alleviate the distress of the entire army, he must relent, as heroes have done in the past:

though no one could blame your anger, not before.
So it was in the old days too. So we've heard
in the famous deeds of fighting men,
of heroes, when seething anger would overcome the great ones.
Still you could bring them round with gifts and winning words (*Iliad* 9.638–642).

Achilles remains unappeased, and warns Phoenix to stop trying to convince him lest the love he feels for him turn to hate. Ajax, Achilles' cousin who is a member of the delegation, tries a different tactic. He reminds Achilles of the accepted custom in heroic society (a custom also attested to by the description of the scenes engraved on the shield that Achilles will receive from Hephaestus after Patroclus' death), according to which even a person whose son or brother has been murdered receives compensation and suffices with that:

> Why, any man will accept the blood-price paid
> for a brother murdered, a child done to death.
> And the murderer lives on in his own country
> the man has paid enough, and the injured kinsman
> curbs his pride, his smoldering, vengeful spirit,
> once he takes the price. (*Iliad* 9.771–777)

Ajax outlines an interesting continuum of social order, positing on one end a social regime based on consent that forestalls successive waves of revenge in cases of violence and murder. The injured parties can suffice with "the blood-price" without paying a social price of shame.[146] In such a social code, revenge is constrained by strict social rules that shape the procedure of retaliation and its limits, thus erecting a certain protective wall against the destructiveness of unending cycles of revenge. At the other end of the continuum is the havoc caused by parties unable to come to an agreement, for whatever cause.

Ajax, too, fails to convince Achilles to move toward a social arrangement of peaceful rather than violent resolution of rage. Although Achilles acknowledges the logic and sense of Ajax's argument, he is unable to control his fury:

> all well said, after my own heart, or mostly so.
> But my heart still heaves with rage (*Iliad* 9.788–789).

Neither stories about past heroes' willingness to compromise, nor custom regarding compensation for a death, which erases even the guilt of murder, nor the pleas of his beloved friends are effective in shielding the Greeks from the fatal effects of Achilles' wrath and the destruction that he unleashes upon them.

In the future, the polis and its rules and regulations, effected through law and its institutions, will enhance the protection of individuals and society both from the consequences of unbounded anger, of "rage" that is "murderous" (Iliad 1.1–2), which is the central topic of the *Iliad*. The generative story of the regimentation of deadly wrath by means of law will emerge in the tragedy gen-

---

146 Cantarella 2001, 477.

rein the *Oresteia*. The court whose establishment will be described there will be lauded as "salvation for your citadel, your land's defense" (*Eumenides* 701).[147] The *Iliad*, however, is a story of the absence of societal defenses against wrath, a deficiency that causes "countless losses, hurling down to the House of Death so many sturdy souls" (*Iliad* 1.2–3).

Odysseus: "Not even then would I stay my hands from slaughter"

Unlike Achilles, Odysseus is not serially wrathful. The epithet most often applied to him by Homer is *polytropus*, which in English has been variously translated as "crafty," "shifty," "adventurous," "ingenious," "restless," "clever," "various minded," "of twists and turns," and so forth.[148] Interestingly, Emily Wilson chose to translate *polytropus* as "complicated,"[149] and indeed Odysseus is a complicated character. With false modesty he presents himself as a man and not a god (*Odyssey* 7.244–245), but the poet depicts him as "a man equipped with the gods' own wisdom" (*Odyssey* 13.101). Years of wandering, facing perils, surmounting obstacles, and overcoming temptations reveal his courage, friendship, compassion and love, but also expressions of cruelty, arrogance, and hatred. Odysseus' actions and responses generally reflect resourcefulness, cunning, practical sense, self-control, and planning: He is skilled in combat, prevarication, deceit, love, entreaties, and manipulation of other people's emotions. He is devoted to his men but does not hesitate to imperil their lives. He is able to accept their loss with relative ease as he moves forward to pursue his next adventure. As Ahrensdorf aptly stated, "Odysseus's character oscillates between prudence and recklessness, pleasure-seeking and glory-seeking, self-restraint and fury, skepticism and piety."[150]

Odysseus also exhibits a wide range of emotions, including wrath. But unlike Achilles' rage, which is placed at the heart of *The Iliad*, Odysseus' anger

---

147 The quotes from *The Eumenides* in this chapter are taken from *Greek Tragedies 3: Aeschylus: The Eumenides; Sophocles: Philoctetes, Oedipus at Colonus; Euripides: The Bacchae, Alcestis*, trans. Richmond Lattimore, eds. Mark Griffith, Glenn W. Most, David Grene and Richmond Lattimore (Chicago: University of Chicago Press, 2013).

148 For details of the translators' choices, see Wyatt Mason, "The First Woman to Translate the 'Odyssey' into English," (New York) *The New York. Times Magazine* (November 2, 2017). (hereinafter abbreviated as: Mason 2017.

149 Mason 2017.

150 Ahrensdorf 2014, 253.

is not framed as the crux of the narrative, and Homer refers to it almost in passing, which may explain why it has received little scholarly attention.[151] It is nonetheless deserving of much closer inspection, for it has significant meaning.

Odysseus' wrath and its consequences come to light in several events. The first is Odysseus' decision to reveal his identity to the cyclops Polyphemus. This decision, Knox suggests, shows that Odysseus shares with Achilles an extreme sensitivity toward what each considers an affront to his honor.[152] Odysseus relied upon the cyclops' hospitality to strangers, but Polyphemus violated the norm and devoured several of Odysseus' traveling companions, dishonoring him and arousing his wrath (*Odyssey* 9.531–536).

Homer does not explicitly clarify whether Odysseus, when he blinds the sleeping cyclops, is acting out of self-defense or out of an angry desire to avenge the breach of *xenia*, the ancient and sacred code of hospitality. In my view, the description of the conclusion of Odysseus' the encounter with the cyclops inclines to the second interpretation. Only when he is at a safe distance, aboard the departing boat, does Odysseus jeer at the wretched, blind cyclops, and divulge his identity. Clearly, choosing to take such action has no purpose other than to vent his anger, and for this choice Odysseus will pay a heavy price. As soon as Polyphemus learns who has injured him, he entreats his father Poseidon for justice:

> grant that Odysseus, raider of cities,
> Laertes' son who makes his home in Ithaca, never reaches home.
> Or if he's fated to see his people once again and reach his well-built house
> and his own native country, let him come home late
> and come a broken man– all shipmates lost,
> alone in a stranger's ship –
> and let him find a world of pain at home! (*Odyssey* 9.588–595)

Polyphemus requests a specific punishment for Odysseus, and even offers an alternative – as is customary in the halls of justice to this day. Poseidon is responsive and the *Odyssey* in its entirety is the outcome of this uncontrolled fit of anger. In effect, it is the story of the trials and tribulations inflicted upon Odysseus because Polyphemus receives his justice. Odysseus might have been spared those travails if he'd controlled his anger, just as the travails brought on by the

---

151 Knox 1996, lvi.
152 Knox 1996, liv.

wrath of Achilles in the *Iliad* might have been prevented if Achilles had suppressed his fury.[153]

A second episode of wrath, which occurs when Odysseus confronts Penelope's suitors, ends in the slaying of Eurymachus. After Odysseus' identity is revealed and he has shot an arrow through Antinous, the suitors' leader, Eurymachus attempts to placate Odysseus. He describes Antinous as having had the most responsibility for the suitors' scandalous behavior, admits that his death was justified, and proposes compensation for the affront to Odysseus' honor in exchange for the lives of the other suitors:

> twenty oxen in value, bronze and gold we'll give
> until we melt your heart. Before we've settled,
> who on earth could blame you for your rage? (*Odyssey* 9.61–62)

Before shooting an arrow at Eurymachus, Odysseus makes it clear that he prefers revenge and retaliation over any sort of compensation.

There is an interesting parallel between what Phoenix says to Achilles in the *Iliad* and Eurymachus' remarks in the *Odyssey*. Their appeals share a similar argumentation strategy. Both admit that initial rage was expected and justified, at least before compensation is offered. Phoenix says to Achilles, "though no one could blame your anger, not before" (*Iliad* 9.638), while Eurymachus tells Odysseus, "Before we've settled, who on earth could blame you for your rage?" (*Odyssey* 22.63–64). In both cases, the speakers base their appeal on the customary social rule that requires the injured and enraged individual to accept an appropriate offer of compensation, otherwise the rage becomes unjustified and reproachable.

Both Achilles and Odysseus utterly reject the appeals to abide with this customary social rule. Achilles refuses to relent no matter how grand the compensation that Agamemnon might offer him:

> not if his gifts outnumbered all the grains of sand
> and dust in the earth – no. not even then could Agamemnon
> bring my fighting spirit round until he pays me back. (*Iliad* 9.470–472)

---

153 Calvin S. Brown, *Reading for the Plot: Design and Intention in Narrative* (New York: A.A. Knopf, 1984), 202 (hereinafter abbreviated as: Brown 1984). Brown draws a parallel between Achilles' wrath and Odysseus' hubris: "He had brought them on himself by that moment of triumph and insolence when he shouted his name to Polyphemus and so laid himself open to the ogre's curse. In the same way that the Iliad is about the wrath of Achilles, the Odyssey is about the hubris of Odysseus."

Odysseus similarly declares that no compensation will sway him from his rage and quest for revenge:

> No, Eurymachus! Not if you paid me all your father's wealth –
> all you possess now, and all that could pour in from the world's end –
> no, not even then would I stay my hands from slaughter
> till all you suitors had paid for all your crimes! (*Odyssey* 22. 65–68)

Both Achilles and Odysseus repudiate the social convention regulating revenge, refusing to submit to its dictates, and in both cases, their unwillingness to submit to the regimentation of anger has horrific effects on society at large.

Any revulsion that the reader feels at Odysseus' display of fury is compounded by the third episode of wrath, which concludes the *Odyssey*. After the massacre of the suitors, their relatives gather to contemplate a violent response. At this stage Athena, who is now inclined to end what she calls "the pain, the cruel fighting" (*Odyssey* 24.525), appeals to Zeus to intervene. Zeus rules that since Odysseus has already taken revenge on the suitors and there is no obstacle that prevents him from returning to the kingship of Ithaca, he should make the relatives forget the slaughter of their sons and brothers. Their amnesia is necessary to allow communal social existence in the future.

Athena proceeds to the battleground, where Odysseus and his company are in the midst of slaughtering their adversaries, and calls for a truce:

> Hold back, you men of Ithaca, back from brutal war!
> Break off – shed no more blood – (*Odyssey* 24.584–585)

Everyone lays down their arms and the suitors' vanquished relatives, who, thanks to Zeus' intervention, have forgotten their duty to avenge the killing of their sons, return to the city. Nonetheless it is at this moment, against the background of his outright victory and Athena's order to cease the hostilities, that Odysseus' fury is re-ignited. He goes back on the offensive:

> the long-enduring great Odysseus,
> gathering all his force, swooped like a soaring eagle – (*Odyssey* 24.590–591)

Zeus is compelled to put on a threatening display to reinforce Athena's demand for a ceasefire. He hurls a lightning bolt wrapped in smoke at Athena's feet. Athena again commands Odysseus to cease the fighting, warning him that if he fails to do so he will arouse Zeus' fury. It is only the threat of this divine anger that finally prompts Odysseus to obey. Athena puts her plan into motion and strikes a peace agreement between the parties. Odysseus' journey thus terminates in an outburst of rage that was controlled only by the direct intervention of Zeus himself.

Are Odysseus' final lethal acts the outcome of his anger? Ahrensdorf seems to think so. He notes, "[t]he Odyssey concludes with Odysseus exhibiting violent anger against the relatives of the suitors he has slain."[154] Yet the complexity of Odysseus' character supports another possibility. His conduct can also be read as the product of cold calculation rather than raging fury. Against the background of his calculating character and practical cunning, his rejection of Eurymachus' offer of compensation and his disregard of Athena's command to lay down his arms may stem not from uncontrollable rage but from his deliberate intention to kill anyone who might pose a threat to him in the future. This interpretative line perceives Odysseus as a ruthless strategist, managing to escape punishment or retribution for killing on a massive scale that was neither proportionate nor necessary. In this spirit, West suggests that Homer must have recognized the problematics of the *Odyssey*'s conclusion:

> He [Homer – S.A] was not happy with an Odyssey in which the hero, after massacring the flower of the local youth, who had indeed abused his property and plotted to kill his son but had not in fact shed any blood, simply resumed his domestic life and his kingship with no questions asked.[155]

Against this background, West suggests that we read the *deus ex machina* episode that concludes the *Odyssey* as a somewhat forced solution that Homer devised as a transition to his final line – the peace agreement that allows Odysseus to pay no price for his profligate butchery.[156]

It may be that Homer felt committed not to stray from the conclusion that was dictated by the myth familiar to his audience. The myth frames the story of the hero's return as a tale of recompense. A man returns to his home after years of enforced absence to discover that ill-meaning suitors have been trying to steal his wife and property from him. Under the aegis of the gods, the return ends successfully, with justified revenge on the ill-wishers. Nonetheless, the agitated events related in the conclusion of the *Odyssey* betrays Homer's discomfort with the intensity and scope of Odysseus' revenge and the fact that Odysseus escapes punishment.

In order to investigate Odysseus' motives, let us take another look at his actions. Do the suitors' conduct and their consequent slaughter *en masse* constitute

---

154 Ahrensdorf 2014, 17.
155 West 2014, 306.
156 West 2014, 306.

a genuine case of "villainy and retribution"?[157] Does the degree of "villainy" exhibited by the suitors justify "retribution" in the form of a death sentence, especially in view of Eurymachus' proposal which, grounded in a well-known social rule and widespread custom, creates an expectation that Odysseus would accept compensation of greater value than what had been taken from him? Furthermore, as Phoenix describes in the *Iliad*, and as emerges from the description of Achilles' shield, it was customary to offer monetary compensation even in the case of murder.

The suitors did not take any life, and while their conduct may have been outrageous and disrespectful to the ruling house, it was quite understandable – even inevitable – under the political circumstances that are described in the first chapter. The enduring uncertainty of whether Odysseus is alive or dead, his son's young age, and the queen's decision to freeze her own status for years created conditions for an unavoidable power struggle in Ithaca. The suitors played out this struggle with arrogance and avarice, doing as they liked with Odysseus' property and his family members. Nonetheless, they act within certain limits. They committed no violence for almost the entire period, only at the very end conspiring to murder Telemachus. They did not harm Odysseus' father Laertes, did not grab power by force, nor did they compel Penelope to marry one of them against her will.

Odysseus' response is however extremely violent. He rejects the offer of compensation and reconciliation, and slaughters almost the entire cadre of Ithaca's elite youth. Additionally, he sentences the serving women of his household suspected of disloyalty to a cruel and humiliating death, despite being told that these women had actually been victims of rape. Melanthius, a servant of the household whose sin was having helped the suitors and insulted the disguised Odysseus, is put to death and his corpse subjected to terrible abuse.

The absolute refusal to accept compensation-reconciliation tells the story, in effect, of a rage that is blameful, to use the terminology that Homer puts in Eurymachus' mouth. Odysseus is to blame on two counts: his rejection of the customary social convention, and the lack of proportionality of his responses – the unbridgeable discrepancy between the sins of the suitors and the serving women and the death sentence that Odysseus imposed on them.

It is difficult to pinpoint the "true motives" of a fictional character, especially a character bursting with internal contradictions such as Odysseus. For our purpose here, it suffices to assert that in either case, whether Odysseus' conduct is ascribed to uncontrolled rage, or to a display of rage designed to camouflage

---

157 According to Finley 1972, 162.

cold political calculation, the story is a cautionary tale of anger conceptualized as a license to kill.

Causality versus Destiny: "Against the will of Fate"

The Homeric epic is a fabric in which threads of choice and divine decree or fate are interwoven, and accorded different degrees of prominence at various junctures of the story's progression. This intricate interlacing of free will and determinism challenges our ability to morally categorize anger in the cases of Odysseus and Achilles and ascribe responsibility for the violence and slaughter that are the products of anger. I turn now to an investigation of this complexity.

Both works reflect tension between a conception of the heroes' actions as the product of choice or as dictated by divine decree or preordained fate. Achilles, as was extensively illustrated, is described as serially enraged. However, should the responsibility for the events described in the *Iliad* be ascribed to his waves of wrath, or to Zeus' intervention in human affairs and his manipulation of Achilles' anger? Is there a direct causal relation between Achilles' choices and the mass deaths of Greeks and Trojans?

The *Odyssey* raises a similar question: If Odysseus' successful return to Ithaca is the product of Fate (whether conceptualized as Zeus' decision or that of the Moirai, to which even the gods are subject),[158] not much importance attaches to the role that anger plays in Odysseus' choices and actions, including his mass slaughter of the suitors. On such a view, Achilles and Odysseus are both pawns in a strategic game played by the gods, and therefore these heroes' conduct in itself serves no purpose in furthering our understanding of proper or improper human behavior. To put the question in other words, to what extent are Achilles and Odysseus free agents who decide on their own actions and may therefore, at least conceptually, bear responsibility for the choices resulting from their outbursts of anger? As James Morrison states, "It is also possible that the will of Zeus includes more broadly the wrath of Achilles, including its cause and effects."[159]

This issue distinctly relates to the understandings of law and justice that emerge from the epics. One of the central tenets of any rule of law is acknowl-

---

[158] For a discussion of the question of the gods' subservience to the dictates of fate, see James V. Morrison, "Kerostasia, The Dictates of Fate, and the Will of Zeus in the Iliad," Arethusa 30.2 (1997): 276–296, 288–292. (hereinafter abbreviated as: Morrison1997).

[159] Morrison 1997, 277. For the various positions regarding whether Homer ascribes free will to his epic heroes, see Morrison 1997, 282.

edgment of the link between the capacity to choose and the responsibility for that choice. To those who lack a genuine capacity to choose, we should not assign responsibility for the outcomes of their actions. It is doubtful whether such a person can serve to efficiently represent narratives of the establishment of justice and rule of law, which are grounded in recognition of the link between one's choice of action and one's responsibility. In order for a legal system to grow, it is vital to acknowledge the existence of the range of alternatives of human conduct, and recognize that each chosen alternative inevitably leads to a distinct outcome. A fatalistic conception that narrows or negates the meaning of choosing among alternative courses of action obstructs the growth of a conception that links choice to responsibility. For Knox, the kernel of the question is this: "Is there, in fact, in Homer, any fully formed concept of free and responsible human action?"[160] Ostensibly, Homer indicates that human action is driven by gods and goddesses. Examples abound. For example, Zeus uses his power to have Agamemnon visited by "a murderous dream" (*Iliad* 2.7), which prompts the Greek commander to make faulty strategic decisions. Also, in Book I, Achilles refrains from attacking Agamemnon physically only because Athena grasps him by the hair and restrains him.

Nonetheless, a penetrating look reveals the complexity that characterizes the question of human responsibility. In Homer's epics, Zeus can send a dream to perturb Agamemnon's sleep, but he cannot be sure of the desired outcome: Agamemnon remains autonomous to a large degree, and he invests thought and calculation, "his heart racing with hopes" (*Iliad* 2.42), and he reconsiders and even consults the elders. Only with their encouragement and approval does he decide to take action in view of the dream. It is interesting that Agamemnon is later described as someone who feels having fallen victim to a manipulation that has deranged his thinking. Zeus, he maintains, planted a "savage madness" (*Iliad* 19.102) is his soul, which caused him to take Briseis from Achilles, thus arousing the latter's wrath.

The description of Achilles' response to the insult hurled at him by Agamemnon also intertwines several elements of agency and choice, besides the physical manner in which Athena restrains him. Immediately before the goddess' intervention, Achilles considers whether to contain his rage or kill Agamemnon, and Athena intervenes before he comes to a decision, "As his racing spirit veered back and forth" (*Iliad* 1.227). Homer leaves us to believe that Achilles might have decided to control his racing spirit even without the goddess's intervention. Fur-

---

160 Knox 1996, iv. For the various scholarly positions regarding the question of the measure of autonomy of the Homeric heroes, see Morrison 1997, 262.

thermore, Athena does not employ the language of command, and does not address him in the imperative. "Down from the skies I come to check your rage if only you will yield" (*Iliad* 1.242–243), she says, seeking to persuade him not to use his sword.

Homer, then, is telling us about a complex manifestation in the framework of which human decision-making may include an element of divine intervention or manipulation, though the latter does not render human discretion redundant. Similar examples of human choice acting in tandem with active intervention by a god or goddess appear in other places in the *Iliad* and the *Odyssey*, constantly representing the tension between Fate and choice.

In the *Odyssey*, for example, Athena disguised as Nestor reveals to Telemachus an interesting detail about Clytemnestra's infidelity. Clytemnestra, she tells him, was an upright woman who rejected Aegisthus' advances, "but the doom of the gods had bound her to surrender" (*Odyssey* 3.307). If Athena is to be believed, the primary reason that Clytemnestra took Aegisthus as her lover was divine decree and not choice. In almost the same breath, however, Athena notes that Clytemnestra agreed to join Aegisthus, who "swept her off to his own house, lover lusting for lover" (*Odyssey* 3.310).

Athena provides another example of manipulatively arousing anger in mortals in order to influence their behavior. When Odysseus disguised as a beggar arrives at the palace, Athena triggers in the suitors an urge to insult and hurt him, so that Odysseus' wrath would be directed against the suitors. To further to this aim, she also caused the suitors to ridicule Telemachus and "set off uncontrollable laughter in the suitors, crazed them out of their minds" (*Odyssey* 20.385–386).

The epics also reveal an additional dimension of tension between Fate's decree and the will of gods or mortals. In the *Odyssey*, Athena describes this tension:

> not even the gods
> can defend a man, not even one they love, that day
> when fate takes hold and lays him out at last. (*Odyssey* 3.269–271)

Such tension is present not only Homer's world. To this day, aphorisms such as "All is foreseen, and freedom of choice is granted,"[161] positing the idea of free will and its attendant responsibility versus hidden constraints on free choice are prevalent in many societies. Returning to Homer, the solutions to this tension proposed by the *Iliad* and the *Odyssey* share several elements. The first, which

---

161 Mishna, Ethics of the Fathers (Pirkei Avot), 3:15.

echoes throughout the narrative, is the acknowledgment that divine intervention and mortals' responsibility for their actions exist side by side. Clytemnestra, then, is fated to submit to Aegisthus' seduction, even as she also chooses to do so, for which she will pay with her life. Athena induces the suitors to behave in an outrageously provocative manner, but they also choose to do so, and pay for it with their lives. In the *Iliad*, Achilles is instrumental in Troy's preordained destruction, but at the same time he makes a series of decisions and chooses among various possibilities throughout the epic. In effect, the crucial events in the narrative stem from his choices, and for these Achilles pays a heavy price.

Another shared element is the constant awareness that what has been fated and predetermined can also change. Again, in both the *Iliad* and the *Odyssey*, there is a sense that the decree of Fate may change, due to either human action or Olympian intervention that diverts the course of events from its preordained conclusion.

In the *Iliad*, the gods' and goddesses' subordination to the decree of Fate is illustrated by the story of the death of Sarpedon, Zeus' beloved son (*Iliad*, Book XVI). Zeus knows that his son is destined to die in combat. He confides in Hera that he is deliberating whether to allow the decree of Fate to be executed, or to save his son. Hera is against intervening: Sarpedon, she tells her husband, is a mortal whose fate was determined long ago. If Zeus should extricate him from the grip of death, other gods and goddesses will want to set aside the decree of Fate and save their children. The result would be terrible discord among the warriors, many of whom are children of immortals, though most are not. Zeus is persuaded and chooses not to intervene, sufficing with precipitating a rainy squall of blood drops in his son's honor.

Homer's Zeus, then, acknowledges in principle his ability to override what has been ordained and to change the decree of Fate. A key statement from his lips comes in the context of his attempt to persuade the gods to actively participate in the fighting between Greeks and Trojans, so as to prevent Achilles from changing the decree of Fate:

> Now, with his rage inflamed for his friend's death,
> I fear he'll raze the walls against the will of fate. (*Iliad* 20.35–36)

Zeus seems to think that the intensity of Achilles' wrath might enable him to breach the walls of Troy, undermining not only the will of Zeus himself but even subverting what had been ordained by Fate. Zeus seeks to neutralize Achilles' potential disruptive power, so he sends the gods and goddesses to join the battle and take action as they choose.

The epic's stance on freedom of choice and its consequences is, then, rather elusive. The decree of Fate is frequently mentioned, yet autonomy is exercised in many episodes. The Homeric heroes incessantly make choices. They choose to take action and to refrain from action, they choose to discuss and explain their decisions, they choose to fight and they choose to kill. The epic is in motion, as Morrison proposed, creating a lively movement between two poles: that of fatalism or preordained fate, and that of free choice:

> The resulting tension between these two poles causes the narrative to shift back and forth, now toward predestination, now toward openness and unpredictability.[162]

Alongside the general notion of divine ordainment or Fate's decree, the Homeric epics juxtapose a close examination of human motives, personal choice, and responsibility for the consequences of choices. Homer's frequent references to Zeus' decrees are understandable from a poetic standpoint. The decrees of gods and Fate are an inseparable part of the mythical world, familiar to both the poet and his audience. Nonetheless, beyond the poetic element, his lingering over choice gives rise to an ethical stance. As Oliver Taplin asserts, the Homeric epics do not allow its heroes to evade responsibility for their actions because "[b]ehavior is seen nonetheless as the outcome of human motivation as well, and as liable to due blame or punishment."[163]

The mythical language in which the epics speak exposes this notion of accountability, although, as Vernant and Vidal-Naquet argue, its heroes are still far from being able to speak in the language of law.[164] Achilles and Odysseus indulge in mass butchery, and society has no legal-like defensive tools. Nonetheless, the epic sketches the link between human choice and human responsibility, and will lead toward the realm of law, where the practical meaning of this link – the responsibility for the choices – takes more formal shape. Tragedy is the genre that will speak the language of law and be constructed of its materials, as noted by Vernant and Vidal-Naquet, who attribute the following quote to Louis Gernet: "[t]he true material of tragedy is the social thought peculiar to the city state, in particular the legal thought which was then in the process of being evolved."[165]

---

162 Morrison 1997, 279. Morrison notes that the use of the terms "fatalism" and "free choice" in the context of the Homeric epics is of course anachronistic and that they can be exchanged for concepts such as openness and flexibility versus rigidity and lack of choice; Morrison 1997, 275.
163 Oliver Taplin, *Homeric Sounding: The Shaping of the Iliad* (Oxford: Clarendon Press, 1992), 208.
164 Vernant and Vidal-Naquet 1981, vii.
165 Vernant and Vidal-Naquet refer to remarks made by Louis Gernet in the framework of an unpublished series of lectures (Vernant and Vidal-Naquet 1981, 3).

Although, as Gernet asserts, legal thought was not yet fully formed in the Homeric epics, the epics nonetheless reflect a new language, distinct from the language of the myths. Orestes seeks revenge for his father's murder, and the Homeric epics deem his solution – murdering his mother and her lover– rightful, deserving of praise and glory. In the *Odyssey*, the disguised Athena uses this episode to instill courage and resolve in young Telemachus' heart:

> Haven't you heard
> what glory Prince Orestes won throughout the world
> when he killed that cunning, murderous Aegisthus,
> who'd killed his famous father? And you, my friend–
> how tall and handsome I see you now– be brave, you too. (*Odyssey* 1.342–346).

The epics' heroes act in accordance with the model exalted by Athena. While both Achilles and Odysseus unhesitatingly choose to kill, and they too gain glory for their choice, the narrative nonetheless plants seeds of doubt regarding the meritorious nature of that glory and the toll society pays for the glorification of its heroes. Hundreds of corpses pile up on Achilles' path to victory on the battlefield. Odysseus advances toward his own glory upon the backs of hundreds of men and women that he has slain or that have died because of him – his crewmates on the journey, Phaeacians who helped him return home, Ithaca's aristocratic elite, and the victimized serving women of his own household. The epics suggest that the conduct that myth frames as heroic exacts a heavy cost from society as a whole. The question whether that price is inescapable resonates powerfully throughout the epic, and therein lay the seeds of a response, which will begin to clearly take shape in the age of tragedy.

Tragedy will emerge toward the end of the sixth century BC. In it, mythical language would be inadequate for the purpose of telling the story of Orestes, whose decision to kill his mother would lead to the establishment of law and criminal justice. The language of myth was no longer relevant to the political reality of the Greek city-state.[166] Myth, especially in the way it manifests in the epics, was still present in collective consciousness, and is represented in various ways through descriptions of the tragic hero's consciousness, yet the solution to the hero's dilemma arrives from a new direction. The narrative answer to Orestes' distress does not originate from the direction memorialized in the epics and recommended by the Homeric Athena – homicide as a means of ensuring eternal glory. The solution that tragedy tells of, orchestrated by Aeschylus' Athena, stems from the new understandings and new values represented by the

---

166 Vernant and Vidal-Naquet 1981, vii.

polis.[167] Supreme among these is the need to defend society against the murderous rage of individuals. The tool to produce such defenses is law. As an institution representing the interests of society at large, the law underscores the disconnect between the personal interest of the mythical hero and the collective interest. While Achilles and Odysseus, who chose to kill, faced no responsibility for their actions and would end up as glorious heroes in cultural consciousness, the fate of Orestes, the tragic hero, would be governed by the new conception that links a choice to kill and the assumption of responsibility for that action. Orestes would be judged by the new institution established by Athena atop the Areopagus, and would end up rescued from a conviction by the skin of his teeth.

The transition from mythical language to the language of tragedy, which is also the language of law, entailed another change. The establishment of law also required a narrative that reflected not only a transformation in mortals' domain but also a change in the ethos of the gods. The next section tracks this change through a discussion of the meaning of Olympian anger in the epics.

Games of the Olympians

The reason for the Trojan War, myth tells us, was a decision made by Zeus and Themis, his second wife and the goddess of justice and social order, to solve the problem of overpopulation in the world by starting a war that would claim the lives of many mortals.[168] Zeus sets the project in motion by arousing the wrath of Eris, the goddess of strife and discord. As a result of Zeus' plotting, Eris is not invited to an important event, the wedding of King Peleus and the nymph Thetis, whose son Achilles would someday play a major role in the course of that war devised atop Mt. Olympus. Eris is, as expected, angered by the rude insult to her honor, and she seeks revenge. At the height of the celebration, Eris tosses a golden apple into the banquet hall, with the words "To the fairest of all" inscribed upon it. The apple performs its discordant function. Each of the three goddesses, Aphrodite, Hera and Athena, lays claim to it, but Zeus, in keeping with his master plan, refuses to decide the matter and refers the goddesses to the judgment of a mortal, Paris, prince of Troy. Each of the goddesses in turn offers Paris a bribe to choose in her favor. Paris accepts the proposal of Aphrodite,

---

167 Vernant and Vidal-Naquet 1981, vii.

168 For details of this myth, its origins, and the reasons for the relatively scant attention devoted to it, see John D. Reeves, The Cause of the Trojan War: A Forgotten Myth Revived," *The Classical Journal* 61.5 (1966): 211–214.

who promises him the most beautiful woman in the world, Helen, daughter of Zeus and Leda. Paris rules that Aphrodite is the fairest of all, and provides one of the earliest examples in cultural history of biased judicial decision-making, corrupted by bribery.

Aphrodite helps Paris abduct Helen from her husband King Menelaus and bring her to his city of Troy. Menelaus gathers together his allies, the greatest warriors of Greece, who set out in a thousand ships to retrieve Helen.[169] The wrath of the two goddesses who lost the contest, Hera and Athena, drives the tragedy of Troy's destruction. It is their anger and not Helen's astounding beauty that sets a thousand ships to sail, and their anger fuels their continued assistance to the Greeks throughout the war and drives their manipulations to discomfit the Trojans.[170] As myth clarifies, all the vicissitudes of the war derive from Zeus' plan. Already in Book I of the *Iliad*, the poet tells us that "the will of Zeus was moving toward its end" (*Iliad* 1.6).

Like ripples spreading out from a pebble tossed into water, once Eris' anger has been tossed into the world, additional waves of wrath radiate from it. Other gods and goddesses enter the fray and take an active part in the raging war, competing in the deadliness of their anger. Poseidon, Zeus' brother, is angry at Troy and determined to destroy it because Laomedon, Priam's father, betrayed his trust and failed to pay for the construction of Troy's walls. Opposing him stands Apollo, who sympathizes with the city that erected an important temple in his honor. Zeus and Hera pull in opposite directions, until Zeus eventually agrees to abandon Troy to Hera's wrath in order to "cure" her of her anger:

> and Priam's sons and the Trojan armies raw
> then you just might cure your rage at last. (*Iliad* 4.41–42)

---

169 An early source for the myth of the Judgment of Paris is the epic poem *Cypria*, attributed to Stasinus, which appears to have been written in the seventh century BC. Many generations later additional versions of the myth were fashioned, the most famous of which are Euripides' plays. For details, see John R. Wilson, "Eris in Euripides," *Greece and Rome* 26.1 (1979): 7–20.

170 Like many other myths that underpin the story and charge it with meaning, the stories of Zeus' fateful decision and the golden apple that aroused the goddesses' wrath are not detailed in *The Iliad*, though allusions in the text indicate that they were familiar to the storyteller and his audience. For a discussion of Homer's regard for the myths and traditions that preceded him, see Laura Slatkin, *The Power of Thetis: Allusion and Interpretation in the Iliad* (Berkeley: University of California Press, 1991), 1–16. For instance, there is a brief reference to the myth of the apple of discord in the final book of *The Iliad*, where it is said that due to Hera and Athena's continuing animosity toward Paris for his championing of Aphrodite, they were opposed to the return of Hector's body to Troy for burial (*Iliad* 23.32–34).

At the same time, though, he forces Hera to accept a reciprocal agreement, which grants Zeus the freedom to exercise his own anger in the future, without any objection on her part:

> Whenever I am bent on tearing down some city
> filled with men you love-to please myself
> never attempt to thwart my fury, Hera,
> give me my way. (*Iliad* 4.47–50)

In the *Iliad*, the gods and goddesses strike agreements and compromises among themselves – as illustrated by this agreement between Zeus and Hera – but are entirely indifferent to the fate or suffering of mortals. How they conduct themselves in the *Iliad* is suggestive of a particularly cruel and violent war game, waged to vent their wrath.

Zeus of the *Iliad* is described as being driven by capricious urges and emotions, and a constant need to boast and demonstrate his power. His character powerfully represents mortal impotence in face of the gods' arbitrariness. Homer puts the words that best capture this helplessness in the mouth of none other than Achilles. Toward the end of the *Iliad*, Achilles advises Priam to adopt a contemplative stance that might ease the great pain that is afflicting them both. Lamentation, he says, is unhelpful:

> There are two great jars that stand on the floor of Zeus's halls
> and hold his gifts, our miseries one, the other blessings.
> When Zeus who loves the lightning mixes gifts for a man,
> now he meets with misfortune, now good times in turn. (*Iliad* 24.615–619)

Zeus, then, holds the key to the good and bad fortunes that befall mortals, and he distributes them in an arbitrary and unpredictable manner. It is best to resign oneself to the inevitability of the bad, counsels Achilles. This sober appreciation leads to a conception of the gods' and goddesses' conduct in the *Iliad* as being devoid of any moral or ethical dimension. It is indeed hard to find any dispositive moral criterion in the rivalries and alliances of the gods and goddesses, or in Zeus' decisions that affect the lives and deaths of mortals. A typical case is when he chooses to champion Hector on the battlefield:

> They held tight as a working widow holds the scales,
> painstakingly grips the beam and lifts the weight
> and the wool together, balancing both sides even,
> struggling to win a grim subsistence for her children.
> So powerful armies drew their battle line dead even till, at last,
> Zeus gave Hector the son of Priam the greater glory. (*Iliad* 12.502–508)

Nonetheless, Zeus later tips the scales and decides on Hector's death, for no specific reason:

> But now for total war,
> bearing down on the other gods, disastrous, massive,
> their fighting-fury blasting loose from opposing camps
> the powers collided! A mammoth clash-the wide earth roared
> and the arching vault of heaven echoed round with trumpets!
> And Zeus heard the chaos, throned on Olympus heights,
> and laughed deep in his own great heart, delighted. (*Iliad* 21.37–43)

Arbitrariness also characterizes the decisions and actions of most of the gods and goddesses. Of special note is the character of Athena in the *Iliad*, so different from Athena the patroness of restraint and protector of the peace in the *Oresteia*. At a certain point in time, at Hector's behest, the warring sides agree to lay down their arms, and to resolve the issue in a contest between Menelaus and Paris. Just as Paris is about to lose, Aphrodite swoops in to intervene on behalf of the man who gave her the victory over two other goddesses. She rescues Paris and carries him off to safety in Troy. Zeus, however, determines that Menelaus is the victor, and that the gods must choose between two alternatives: "do we rouse the pain and grisly fighting once again, or hand down pacts of peace between both armies?" (*Iliad* 4.17–18). Although she says nothing, Athena is "seized with wild resentment" (*Iliad* 4.26), and is therefore unwilling to hear of any reconciliation between Greeks and Trojans. She arrives at the battlefield disguised as a man, and entices the archer Pandarus to shoot an arrow at Menelaus. Although Menelaus suffers a minor injury from which he quickly recovers, in seconds Athena manages to shatter the possibility of a bloodless resolution of the conflict. It is Athena's wild fury that demands to have killing, and wanton slaughter is what it begets.

In the *Odyssey*, Homer shows us a different Athena. She is often moved by powerful emotions, but wrath is only one of them.[171] She exhibits compassion, affection, and sympathy to Odysseus and those close to him. When her anger is aroused in the *Odyssey*, it does not stem from injured pride. It is triggered by the suitors who are acting against her protégé's interests, and is channeled toward a single goal: helping Odysseus return to Ithaca, by any means necessary. Athena is not alone. There is almost an absolute consensus atop Olympus on the desire to help Odysseus. In contrast to the disputes, arguments, and contrary po-

---

171 For details on how Athena's wrath and its pacification move the story of the *Iliad*, see Strauss-Clay 1983, 213–239.

sitions of the gods and goddesses in the *Iliad*, the gods and goddesses in the *Odyssey*, with one important exception, consider Odysseus deserving of their collective assistance; therefore, they all must contribute to the collective effort to ensure his return.

Is it just reward or divine whim that carries Odysseus back home? The opening lines frame the *Odyssey* as a story of reward for the good and just punishment for the bad. These lines reference several incidents of retributive punishment: Odysseus' men who ate the flesh of the cattle of the sun god Helios were struck down, and Aegisthus, who stole Agamemnon's wife and then murdered him, was murdered in turn by Orestes. In contrast, Odysseus is deserving of assistance in his struggle for his life and the lives of his men because of his generous sacrifices to Zeus and his high-minded aspiration to return to his home and his wife. The gods, led by Zeus and Athena, come together to assist Odysseus, posing a (mostly) united front that seems to be guided by a theory of desert.

In light of the gods' and goddesses' rational conduct in the *Odyssey*, which contrasts their dangerous outbursts of anger in the *Iliad*, the accepted understanding that the *Odyssey* represents a turn toward law, justice and morality is plausible. West, for example, writes that "The gods in the Odyssey show a collective concern for morality that they lack in the Iliad."[172] A striking example of this transition is the Olympian decision to help Odysseus as opposed to their decision to refrain from helping Hector, even though he was also deserving of such assistance by virtue of his qualities of character and the many sacrifices he made to Zeus.[173] The *Odyssey* does appear to be a story that suppresses the malice or arbitrariness attributed to the gods and goddesses in the *Iliad*, highlighting all of them as a collective body, and Zeus in particular, representing a principle of retributive justice. Nonetheless, Homer also presents cases in which the actions of the gods and goddesses lead to the opposite outcome.

Let me begin with Poseidon, the single Olympic god whose actions conform to the principles of retributive justice. Poseidon of the *Odyssey* is, to a large degree, the counterpart of Achilles in the *Iliad*. Just as Achilles' wrath is the driver of the *Iliad*, Poseidon's anger is the driving force of the *Odyssey*. In both works, their respective rage is mentioned in the opening lines, alluding to its focal role in the unfolding events to come: "then every god took pity, all except Poseidon. He raged on [...]" (*Odyssey* 1.22–23). As Charles Segal notes, Poseidon's anger

---

172 West 2014, 48.
173 West 2014, 48.

represents the pursuit of a personal vendetta:[174] Odysseus has blinded Poseidon's son, and Poseidon relentlessly seeks revenge.

Since Poseidon's wrath emerges as the antipode to the principled Olympian outlook, the question arises as to whether we can identify in the *Odyssey* hints of moral sensibility among the gods, in the direction of progress toward justice and the rule of law. According to Segal, positing the possibility that Poseidon is framed as the exception, symbolizing the fading old world, as opposed to Zeus and the other gods who represent progress toward the sphere of law. In order to demonstrate the struggle between the two worlds, Homer brings into confrontation gods with varying degrees of moral sensibility. Poseidon is assigned the role of the angry "Other," and Zeus represents the leader seeking to establish the principle of retributive justice.[175] A close reading nonetheless imparts the sense that the difference between the angry "Other" god and the rational, justice-seeking gods and goddesses is not as dramatic as the opening lines of the *Odyssey* would have us believe.

What first strikes the eye is the discrepancy between the actions of the transgressors, whose sins open the *Odyssey*, and the punishment meted to them. Odysseus' men ignore the warnings and eat the flesh of Helios' cattle after the provisions on their ship run out. Their fear of starvation outweighs their fear of Helios' wrath. Odysseus withstands the temptation of the Sirens by tying himself to the ship's mast and plugging his ears with wax, but when his men need his leadership and supervision, Odysseus abandons them to fend for themselves. Despite the sailors' extenuating circumstances, Helios bursts out "in rage" (*Odyssey* 12.404) in an appeal to the other gods, and rather easily extracts a promise from Zeus to smash the ship in which Odysseus and the cattle-eaters are sailing. Zeus himself strikes the ship with lightning, and everyone aboard except for Odysseus comes to a grisly end. They will not arrive home. This case, which is framed by the poet as an act of stupidity and frivolity (*Odyssey* 1.9), evolves into a representation of justified wrath and retribution.

Zeus' further complicity with another god's wrath, which exacts a terrible price from those whose only sin was their assistance to Odysseus, is described in Book XIII. These are the Phaeacians, who also disregard a divine warning, in this case from Poseidon, who has declared that he opposes any effort to help the mortals reach their destination. King Alcinous ignores the warning and assigns a Phaeacian ship to take Odysseus safely back to his homeland. Un-

---

174 Charles Segal, "Divine Justice in the Odyssey: Poseidon, Cyclops, and Helios," *The American Journal of Philology* 113.4 (1992): 489–518, 510 (hereinafter abbreviated as: Segal 1992).
175 Segal 1992, 490–491.

surprisingly Poseidon is enraged, and demands not only that the Phaeacian ship be destroyed, but that their entire city be buried under a towering mountain. Zeus adds a touch of cruelty to Poseidon's proposal, and suggests turning the ship into stone within site of the shore. If Poseidon's intention is to bury all of Scheria under a towering mountain, Zeus has no problem with that: He endorses Poseidon's anger rather than the Phaeacians' norm of hospitality. Poseidon gladly agrees to this twist, and before the Phaeacians' horrified eyes the ship turns to stone as soon as it reaches its home port. Anger overrules social manners.

Zeus' conduct is particularly galling in light of the fact that he has no reason to harbor any ill-will or anger toward the Phaeacians. On the contrary, the Phaeacians took action courageously and generously to advance the very same cause that he himself is comitted to advance – Odysseus' return to his home. In light of the retributive position that Zeus purports to represent throughout the *Odyssey*, we would expect him to protect the Phaeacians from Poseidon's wrath. But Zeus chooses to limit his intervention, and suffices with suggesting a minor adjustment of the way in which they die.

The text does not clarify whether the entire city was ultimately buried under a mountain, or whether the Phaeacians' prayers and sacrifices saved it from this misfortune. To end the story, the poet references the king's plan to make sacrifices to Poseidon and pray for his mercy. What is clear, however, is that Poseidon's wrath, sanctioned by Zeus, leads to the brutal demise of those who aided Odysseus.[176]

So, then, even if the *Odyssey* ostensibly inclines toward an explicit theory of justice and the principle that "Sinners are, in the end, punished; the final triumph of Odysseus is a triumph of goodness over evil,"[177] it concurrently tells a story that works against such a theory. Beneath the surface of the *Odyssey*, which supposedly marks a new era of liberation from the arbitrariness of that anger, the motif of brutal divine anger that cruelly and arbitrarily strikes down mortals, all too familiar from the *Iliad*, is evident. Against this intricate background, not only is it difficult to see the *Odyssey* as an early manifestation of the striving toward a principle of justice, but it can even be read as a tale of terrible human vulnerability and helplessness, no less chilling and menacing than the *Iliad* itself.

---

176 For details of the Phaeacians' fate, see Rainer Friedrich, "Zeus and the Phaeacians: Odyssey 13.158," *The American Journal of Philology* 110.3 (1989): 395–399.
177 Griffin 2004, 47.

Conclusion

Simone Weil reads the *Iliad* as a text that is mainly concerned with violence.[178] In her powerful and widely acclaimed essay "The Iliad or the Poem of Force," which was written against the backdrop of the horrors of World War II, she describes the *Iliad* as a work that first and foremost exposes its audience to the destructive nature of great power: "The true hero, the true subject matter, the center of the Iliad is force. The force that men wield, the force that subdues men, in the face of which human flesh shrinks back."[179] Although she does recognize rare moments of grace in the *Iliad* – moments of love, friendship, and devotion – all they can arouse as far as she is concerned is acute pain at what violence has already razed and what it will destroy in the future.[180]

In an essay written at much the same dark time against the background of which Weil identified the terror of force at the heart of the *Iliad*, Rachel Bespaloff identifies a different core in the text.[181] In her essay "On the Iliad,"[182] she describes the work as a song of praise for the human ability to choose, to resist, to dare to challenge, and as a derivative of all these, praise for the human ability to enact laws on the foundation of a striving toward an ideal of justice. What emerges and stands out against the gods' and goddesses' plotting and scheming is the greatness of the human spirit, one of the most striking achievements of which is the law:

> Although the gods are involved in the unfolding of events [...] the whole business of founding and building, rising and daring, remains in the hands of man. Law is altogether a human work [...] The gods bestow happiness, wealth, and glory. Man alone has the power to unite them to justice.[183]

---

178 Simone Weil, "The Iliad, or the Poem of Force," in *War and the Iliad*, eds. Simone Weil, Rachel Bespaloff and Hermann Broch, trans. Mary McCarthy (New York, NY: New York Review Books, 2005), 1–37, 1.(hereinafter abbreviated as: Weil 2005)

179 Weil 2005, 3. For details regarding the analogy between what Europe faced at the end of World War II and the crisis described in the *Iliad*, see Christopher Benfey, "Introduction: A tale of two Iliads," in *War and the Iliad*, eds. Simone Weil, Rachel Bespaloff and Hermann Broch, trans. Mary McCarthy (New York, NY: New York Review Books, 2005), vii–xxiii, vii. (hereinafter abbreviated at Benfey 2005.)

180 Weil 2005, 30.

181 The two essays were first placed beside each other in a book in 2005, along with an illuminating survey of the biographical parallels relating to the two authors. See Benfey 2005, vii.

182 Rachel Bespaloff, "On the Iliad," in *War and the Iliad*, eds. Simone Weil, Rachel Bespaloff and Hermann Broch, trans. Mary McCarthy (New York, NY: New York Review Books, 2005), 39–100, 39. (hereinafter abbreviated as Bespaloff 2005.)

183 Bespaloff 2005, 140.

According to Weil, the *Iliad* illustrates everything that violence makes impossible, yet according to Bespaloff, what emerges and stands out from the story of war and death is the redemptive ability to choose. I would argue, however, that the two readings are complementary and not as incompatible as they might initially seem. In both the *Iliad* and the *Odyssey*, the element of force and the element of choice coalesce to synergistically create a heightened representation of societal threat. Through the prism of force, the *Iliad* is the story of a violent society in which might is right, and wrath and arbitrariness constantly exact a toll in the form of human lives, with no redemptive horizon offered by the prism of choice. Although the choices made by men and women are highlighted throughout the epic, choices resort to force in most of the episodes that are significant to advancing the plot. In most choices, it is violence that is chosen. The gods choose to kill people because they are angry. Mortals choose to kill men and women because they prefer to indulge in wrath.

It is tempting to locate and identify in the *Iliad* moments when mortals choose compassion and generosity, and to attribute a constitutive value to them. It is also tempting to delineate a course of moral development from the *Iliad* to the *Odyssey*, a path that marks gradual progress toward a society that accepts subservience to law and to its underlying principles of morality and justice. Nonetheless, what a holistic reading of the Homeric epics brings out first and foremost is human vulnerability.

In the absence of restraint in the form of regimentation and protection, both force and choice are equally dangerous. The epics shout out this inadequacy. As Segal suggests, the *Odyssey* can be read as "[a] tale of divine wrath, cruelty, injustice, non-rationalized and non-moralized misfortune."[184] A similar reading of the *Iliad* seems equally tenable. Yet, Segal adds, "[t]he poem we are hearing exists as the negation of such a tale."[185] In other words, the epics weave a powerful cautionary narrative, revealing the terrible consequences of the freedom to choose force, and the need for a different form of social existence. The story of a society lacking defenses against the rampaging of anger prompts a move toward the regimentation of anger and the development of "protective walls for country and city" (*Eumenides* 701) in the form of criminal justice and the rule of law.

At a later time, with the transition from the epic era to the tragic, the *Oresteia* would present a new narrative, in which both mortals and gods renounce the freedom to give free rein to their anger, and accept its juridification. From the

---

184 Segal 1992, 517.
185 Segal 1992, 517.

myth centering on the deleterious effects of unregimented anger, the generative story of the growth of law would come to be distilled. The Homeric epics are stories about the unacceptable price of anger, while the *Oresteia* tells of how law was born out of anger and acknowledgment of the need for its regimentation. The *Odyssey* and the *Iliad* are thus an inseparable part of the sometimes hesitant and slow rally toward the establishment of law and criminal justice.

To be established, the law would regiment anger and revenge and purport to erect "protective walls for country and city," as promised by Athena, the patroness of law (*Eumenides* 701), but as the future will show, the law's promise would not be fully realized. Although generations of history will show that the law does not always prove itself as an efficient and reliable mechanism of truth-finding, conflict resolution, or justice, its absence – as the Homeric epics reiterate – is categorically unbearable.

Chapter 4
The *Metis Syndrome:* Women and Law in the *Odyssey*

Athena was the daughter of Zeus and Metis,
Ocean's daughter, who knew more than gods or men.
(Caption, New Acropolis Museum, Athens)

The Feminine Spectrum of Action in the Epics

The *Odyssey* is the story of the heroic and trouble-plagued return journey of its hero, Odysseus, to his homeland of Ithaca. That journey is set in motion and advanced by several women without whose initiative, involvement, and support, Odysseus would never have succeeded in returning to Ithaca, let alone restoring his kingship. As I propose here, the female presence described in the *Odyssey* speaks to what I call the *Metis Syndrome.* The ancient myth of Metis, mother of the goddess Athena, is reflected in the Homeric epic as a complex dynamic balance that affords women a relatively broad spectrum of action. In the future, when society gives rise to formal justice, whose emergence is immortalized in Greek tragedy, specifically in the *Oresteia,*[186] such spectrum of female action will be blocked. The *Oresteia* is an exemplar of the growing constraints on women's agency and freedom of choice.

According to the reading proposed here, the *Odyssey* marks an important point on the continuum of the conflict between men and women. The *Oresteia,* the narrative focused on the establishment of rule of law in the Greek world, tells the story of women's defeat in this battle. The establishment of a system of criminal justice yielding to the masculine interest is the decisive resolution at the heart of the *Oresteia,* and marks a significant distance from the pre-rule of law in the time of the *Odyssey,*[187] when both men and women are seemingly free

---

186 For more on the subject, see Shulamit Almog, "From the Odyssey Onwards: Law's Long and Winding Road," *Law & Literature* 32.1 (2002): 47–74 (hereinafter abbreviated as: Almog 2020).
187 Although, as put in previous chapters, Homeric society subjects itself to an intricate web of rules and customs that echo what today would suggest principles of private and public law. Additionally, the culminating crisis in the *Odyssey* ends with the signing of an alliance that has a quasi-judicial dimension. The establishment of formal criminal justice as described in the *Oresteia* is manifested by the appearance of initial judicial elements, substantive and procedural, which exist to the present day. In the plays, reaching a judicial decision involves, as it does

https://doi.org/10.1515/9783110766110-006

to manage their affairs with no regard to any external law. In the narrative of the *Odyssey*, the capacity of women to persuade, convince, and influence is always at play, and they have significant control over their destinies.

An important qualification is warranted. Although the *Odyssey*'s plot gives women a central place, the society it portrays is distinctively androcentric,[188] where the masculine view, masculine will, and masculine interests prevail.[189] Nonetheless, the reality that emerges from the *Odyssey* is such that allows women, in many cases, to break through the barriers imposed by the androcentric social order, and to take action in ways that significantly impact not only their own destinies but those of men as well. As I elaborate in this book, one of the central enabling factors of this situation is the general commitment of the society described in the *Odyssey* to conceptions of justice, and to social life governed by rules, albeit without a fixed formal framework of rule of law. The *Oresteia*, written hundreds of years later in reference to the Heroic Age, the same era as the *Odyssey*, tells a fundamentally different story of women's agency, a story in which women are much more firmly subservient to masculine hegemony and interests. As emerges from the *Oresteia*, the elaboration of the rule of law did not significantly constrain the androcentric conception of society, yet I argue that it reduced and even obstructed the partial female agency reflected in the Homeric epics.

---

today, a public trial, which is designed to ensure the procedural fairness. For elaboration see Chapter 1.

188 For a definition of the term androcentric, see Lindsay Jones and Gale Group, *Encyclopedia of Religion*, 2nd ed. (Detroit: Macmillan Reference, 2005), 334.

189 Froma I. Zeitlin, *Playing the Other: Gender and Society in Classical Greek Literature* (Chicago: University of Chicago Press, 1996) (hereinafter Zeitlin 1996); Lillian Eileen Doherty, *Siren Songs: Gender, Audiences, and Narrators in the Odyssey* (Ann Arbor: University of Michigan Press, 1995) (hereinafter abbreviated as Doherty 1995). As Froma Zeitlin says regarding the status of women in the Odyssey, "That an apparent symmetry appears in the pairing of male/female does not disguise the fundamental, even disabling, asymmetry in status, rank, and power or focus of interest and influence. No amount of wishful thinking ... [can] redress the serious imbalance" (Zeitlin 1996, 7). I adopt Zeitlin's preference for the term "androcentric society" to describe the ancient Greek society reflected in the myths over the term "patriarchal society," which in her eyes is both too narrow and too broad to capture the complexity of this society in terms of the spectrum of action open to women. Lillian Doherty also chooses to avoid using the term "patriarchal" when analyzing manifestations of gender in the *Odyssey* and to use in its place the term "androcentric." The former term, she explains, is narrower, referring to the monopoly on political power held by adult males. The latter term more faithfully describes the state of Homeric society: "Norms, narrative patterns, and other thought structures that give priority to male subject positions – that is, that posit a male, or male identified, figures as the point of reference" (Doherty 1995, 5).

The chapter proceeds as follows: First I introduce the myth of Metis and the *Metis Syndrome* that derives from it. The *Metis Syndrome* represents the perpetual masculine suspicion of women's wile and cunning, which leads to their violent obstruction of women, and sometimes even women's murder. On the feminine side, the *Metis Syndrome* expresses a female consciousness of the danger that a demonstration of their abilities entails, alongside the judicious and covert use of these abilities. Next I trace the manifestations of the *Metis Syndrome* in the protagonists of the *Odyssey*. In the part devoted to Odysseus' wife Penelope, the *Metis Syndrome* is helpful in clarifying puzzling aspects of the *Odyssey*'s enigmatic leading female protagonist. Following sections address Calypso and Circe, two descendants of Titans whose characters suggest that the feminine ability to evade patriarchal dominance carries a heavy toll: exile and isolation. I also focus on Arete and Nausicaa, respectively queen and princess of an exceptional kingdom that allows them to act as they choose, under the guise of obedience to androcentric norms. The *Odyssey* also tells the story of the servant women who try, and for a short while succeed, in breaking through the confines of gender and status. The price they pay – their lives – echoes the fate of Metis. I conclude with an analysis of the character of Athena in the *Odyssey*, arguing that she is closer to ideals of justice and equality than the Athena of Greek tragedy in significant ways.

I argue that the women of the *Odyssey* – goddesses and mortals, highborn queens and lowly servants – are able to demonstrate autonomy of will and action *because* the society described in the *Odyssey* lacks a template of formal rule of law. Such a template will emerge generations later, in Greek tragedy, marking women's defeat in the struggle for equality.

Metis

The foundation of Greek mythology is an intergenerational and gender struggle between fathers and sons and between the feminine and masculine. The myth concerning the circumstances of the goddess Athena's birth, as well as her various character traits described in ancient sources, is related to this struggle. As recounted by Hesiod in the *Theogony*,[190] out of Chaos emerged several entities,

---

190 Hesiod, who lived until circa the end of the seventh century BC, collected the ancient myths that were known in his time in the *Theogony*, which can be read as ""[a]n account of the gradual shift of power in the cosmos from female to the male" (Eva Stehle, "Sappho's Gaze: Fantasies of a Goddess and Young Man," in *Reading Sappho: Contemporary Approaches*, ed. Ellen Green (Berkeley, CA: University of California Press, 1996). 193–225, 207) (hereinafter abbreviated as Stehle

including Gaia, the Earth. Out of Gaia were formed the Ocean, the mountains, and the sky – Uranus. Gaia mated with her son Uranus, and the two of them produced the first generation of gods – the Titans. Uranus, who feared them, hid them away inside Gaia's enormous body. Pained, Gaia persuaded her younger son Kronos to rebel against his father and created a scythe for him, which he used to castrate Uranus. From Uranus' blood were born the Erinyes, the goddesses of vengeance who pursue those who murder their parents.[191] Kronos mated with Gaia's sister Rhea but swallowed all the children born to him for fear that one of them might depose him. Rhea intervened and hid her youngest son, Zeus, from his father. When Zeus came of age, he waged a war against Kronos and defeated him, liberating his five siblings, Poseidon, Hades, Hera, Demeter, and Hestia, who constituted the first group of gods. After another round of fighting, the intergenerational struggle ended in Zeus' victory.

In the myth, this victory is described as the triumph of patriarchal order over chaos. Both represent the victory of justice.[192] On such a view, Zeus is the great father of the rule of law. His victory symbolizes the termination of the violent patterns that characterized the previous generations – fathers and sons murdering each other, and mothers scheming for their lives and for the lives of their offspring. Zeus ushers in a new era of order and legality – a legality that is determined by men and that first and foremost serves their interests and their continued dominion.

The victory of the new social order is portrayed in myth as a masculine victory over the subversive potential lurking in women's power to give birth. Zeus' sovereignty is the outcome of generations of violent struggles against women's fertility. A similar pattern emerges when Thetis and Ocean, the offspring of Uranus and Gaia, begat Metis, whose name means wisdom, profound thought, and

---

1996). The dating of the *Theogony* as opposed to that of the *Odyssey* remains undecided. For discussion of this question and whether the myth described in the *Theogony* was known also to the author of the *Odyssey*, see Norman O. Brown, "The Birth of Athena," *Transactions and Proceedings of the American Philological Association* 83 (1952): 130–143, 140–143 (hereinafter abbreviated as: Brown 1952). For an English translation of the *Theogony*, see "The Theogony," in *Hesiod, The Homeric Hymns, and Homerica, by Homer and Hesiod*, ed. and trans. Hugh G. Evelyn-White 2008 (1914) (hereinafter: *The Theogony*).

191 For more on this, see Sarah B. Pomeroy, *Goddesses, Whores, Wives, And Slaves: Women in Classical Antiquity* (New York: Knopf Doubleday Publishing Group, 2011), 1–4. Also see Bonnie MacLachlan, *Women in Ancient Greece: A Sourcebook* (London: Continuum, 2012), 1–4. In later times, the Erinyes would return to center stage in the myth in the context of the establishment of the rule of law, in Aeschylus' *Oresteia*.

192 Eva Stehle, *Performance and Gender in Ancient Greece: Nondramatic Poetry in Its Setting* (Princeton, NJ: Princeton University Press, 1997), 207.

practical cunning.[193] Due to these traits, Metis not only counseled Zeus in his struggle against Kronos, but was also a decisive factor in Zeus' victory. It was Metis who revived the children swallowed by Kronos – a potion she brewed made him vomit them back into the world.[194] However, when Metis becomes Zeus' wife after the latter's victory, their relationship is transformed. From that point on, in Zeus' mind, she becomes a double threat. The first threat emanates from Metis' cleverness, which she potentially can employ against Zeus. The second threat is her ability to pass on her power to their children, who would then be strong enough to depose Zeus from his throne. As a precaution, Zeus outwits Metis and uses a ruse to swallow her, absorbing her essence and her wisdom.[195] In this way Zeus averted the first threat, but he was unaware that Metis was pregnant when he swallowed her.[196] The fetus in her womb was Athena. When it came time for her to emerge into the world, Athena hatched out of Zeus' head. From the moment of her birth, the myth describes Athena as the offspring of a single parent, Zeus. Consequently, in the myth in her own eyes she is motherless.[197] Her motherless status reinforces the special bond between Athena and her father and effectively neutralizes Metis' second threat. Athena is Zeus' favorite offspring, and she epitomizes his wisdom and power, but in subservience to him and unconditional acceptance of his authority.

Athena's motherless status and having been born from her father's head assumes major significance in the project of establishing the rule of law. In any case, the myth concerning her devoured mother creates an intricate dynamic that has the capacity to sustain contradicting perceptions.[198] For example, the Metis myth might be understood as support for an ideology centered on male superiority that imposes order, determines how the world is run, and dictates female inferiority. At the same time, this myth allows and even invites a reading that challenges the legitimacy of the masculine power grab. The myth describes this new order as violent, cruel, disturbing, and unjust. Metis, the wise counselor whose assistance was critical to Zeus' victory, and who even married him and

---

193 For more on how the myth resonates and the importance of wisdom/cunning in the ancient Greek world, see Marcel Detienne and Jean-Pierre Vernant, *Cunning Intelligence in Greek Culture and Society*, trans. Janet Lloyd (Chicago; London: University of Chicago Press, 1991), 1–54.

194 For elaboration see Jay Dolmage, "Metis, Mêtis, Mestiza, Medusa: Rhetorical Bodies across Rhetorical Traditions," *Rhetoric Review* 28.1 (2009): 1, 1–28. (hereinafter, Dolmage 2009).

195 *The Theogony* 886–900.

196 *The Theogony* 886–900.

197 In the *Oresteia* Athena uses what she knows about the circumstances of her birth in order to support Orestes' acquittal: "for there is no mother who gave birth to me [...] and [I] am very much my father's child." See *Eumenides* 736–738.

198 For an analysis of the complexity of myths, see Zeitlin 1996, 118–119.

carried his child, is deprived not only of her right to share in the fruits of victory, but is also effectively denied any role in future events.

The transgression at the center of Metis' story invites feminist readings, and it has indeed drawn the attention of scholars who see it as a marker of both women's oppression and female resistance. Lillian Doherty formulates the aspiration "to free Metis" from her eternal prison inside Zeus' body as a metaphor for a gendered reading of the *Odyssey*.[199] Amy Richlin analyzes the swallowing of Metis as a violent appropriation of women's childbearing ability perpetrated by Zeus.[200] Jay Dolmage points to versions of the myth in which Zeus appropriated not only Metis' childbearing ability, but also her practical wisdom and expressive facility. Zeus was unwilling to share his power with his sagacious wife, but neither would he deny himself her services. After he swallowed her, his wise counselor was encased in his own body, and he continued to hear her voice and suggestions emanating from within him, and to use her rhetoric as if it was his.[201] The result, according to Dolmage, was the sweeping subjugation of the feminine: "Metis was wrested from the feminine, its lineage became unofficial, and its uses were coopted and controlled by Zeus."[202]

Using psychoanalytical tools, Amber Jacobs analyzes Metis' disappearance from the later Greek corpus of myth and the absence of any mention of her in the tragedies of Aeschylus, Sophocles, and Euripides.[203] I would suggest that this exclusion is related to the way in which law and particularly criminal justice would come to be shaped in Greek society, and subsequently also in human society in general. The belief in a man's ability to give birth to progeny underpinned Orestes' acquittal and the nature of law from that point onward.[204] A powerful illustration is the expunction of the Metis myth and the scarce attention devoted to it, which occasioned a prolonged silence and enduring lacuna in law and discourse with respect to matricide, "a situation in which matricide remains untheorized and cannot deliver its underlying law."[205]

---

199 Doherty 1995, 8.

200 Amy Richlin, *Zeus and Metis: Foucault, Feminism, Classics* (Lubbock, TX: Texas Tech University Press, 1991).

201 Dolmage 2009, 9.

202 Dolmage 2009, 8.

203 Amber Jacobs, "Towards a Structural Theory of Matricide: Psychoanalysis, the Oresteia and the Maternal Prohibition," *Women: A Cultural Review* 15.1 (2004): 19–34, 24 (hereinafter abbreviated as Jacobs 2004).

204 Jacobs 2004, 32.

205 Jacobs 2004, 25.

Today, when the struggle over the use of female fertility is regimented by law, and when surrogacy, into which women are often forced due to hardship or difficult life circumstances, is becoming a commonplace phenomenon,[206] the myth of Metis – the mother who was eliminated so that someone else could take control of her fertility and possess her child – becomes charged with another layer of meaning. The voice of Metis, an unwilling surrogate who was cruelly suppressed by the mythical figure who stands as the forefather of justice, law and order, expresses the pain of women's oppression and the interminable threat of the forced appropriation of feminine assets and abilities. Metis was swallowed but her story endures and continues to demand the voice, power, and justice that she was denied. The persistence of this myth over time is the *Metis Syndrome*.

The term *Metis Syndrome* is used to denote both feminine power and the survival instinct that prompts women to disguise their power. The *Metis Syndrome* is the female inclination to behave cautiously, diminishing and disguising abilities and skills that might be considered a threat to men. On the male side, the *Metis Syndrome* denotes men's primal fear of women and their perpetual inherent threat to male superiority, a fear that leads men to silence women's voices and abilities, occasionally through the use of violence.

Indications of the male *Metis Syndrome* are evident throughout the *Odyssey*. One indication of major import appears in Book XI, in the conversation between Agamemnon and Odysseus in the Land of the Dead. Agamemnon turns his murder at the hands of his wife Clytemnestra into a crime perpetrated by all women. Clytemnestra comes to represent the danger posed by every woman *qua* woman. And Odysseus amplifies this understanding in an allusion to Metis' assistance to Zeus (which Odysseus derogatorily calls "wiles"):

> How terrible!
> Zeus from the very start, the thunder king
> has hated the race of Atreus with a vengeance
> his trustiest weapon women's twisted wiles (*Odyssey* 11.493 – 496).

Odysseus proceeds to implicate Clytemnestra in the discourse of wiles as the one who set a trap for Agamemnon in his absence. Agamemnon concludes the discussion of the dangers posed by wives with a general warning and a practical suggestion: "So even your wife – never indulge her too far. Never reveal the whole truth, whatever you may know [...]" (*Odyssey* 11.500 – 501).

---

206 For a critique of the contemporary practice of surrogacy from this perspective, see Renate Klein, *Surrogacy: A Human Rights Violation* (North Melbourne, Vic.: Spinifex Press, 2017).

According to Agamemnon, even Odysseus' wife Penelope who is "steady" and "wise" (*Odyssey* 11.504–505) cannot be trusted, and Odysseus is cautioned to arrive at Ithaca in secret:

> I tell you this – bear it in mind, you must
> when you reach your homeland steer your ship
> into port in secret, never out in the open [...]
> the time for trusting women's gone forever! (*Odyssey* 11.515–518).

Odysseus accepts Agamemnon's advice, and for quite a while after his arrival he conceals his identity from Penelope. Men's incessant distrust of female fidelity also motivates Telemachus. When Athena, disguised as a stranger, asks him whether he is the son of Odysseus, Telemachus is not content with a simple affirmation of his identity, feeling impelled to add the following reservation:

> Mother has always told me I'm his son, it's true,
> but I am not so certain. Who, on his own,
> has ever really known who gave him life? (*Odyssey* 1.248–250)

Athena herself is described as implanting in Telemachus' mind a constant fear of women, including a fear of his own mother. While Telemachus visits Menelaus and Helen in Sparta, Athena delivers a message to him, emphasizing the need for his swift return home for fear of Penelope's inability to withstand the pressure of her father and brothers, who are urging her to choose Eurymachus, a wealthy suitor who is showering her with particularly expensive gifts. In such a situation, Athena tells Telemachus, Penelope cannot be trusted, just as women in general cannot be trusted:

> You know how the heart of a woman always works:
> she likes to build the wealth of her new groom –
> of the sons she bore, of her dear, departed husband,
> not a memory of the dead, no questions asked. (*Odyssey* 15.23–26)

The male *Metis Syndrome* – constant male vigilance against female treachery – is prominent in the *Odyssey*,[207] yet a more central place in the narrative is occupied

---

207 Emily Wilson, "A Translator's Reckoning with the Women of the Odyssey," *New Yorker*, December 8, 2017. In this context, Emily Wilson mentions: "The Odyssey traces deep male fears about female power, and it shows the terrible damage done to women, and perhaps also to men, by the androcentric social structures that keep us silent and constrained."

by the female *Metis Syndrome*, the manifestations of which are addressed in the following sections.

Penelope

When Penelope enters the story, she is weeping (*Odyssey* 1.336), and she goes on weeping throughout the epic. Again and again, she cries, moans, sobs, or sighs. The formal reason for Penelope's weeping is her yearning for her absent husband. Penelope spends two decades caring for her son and is doing her best to rebuff dozens of assertive suitors. In the course of the final years of the *Odyssey*' narrative, she resorts to the famous stratagem of weaving a burial shroud for Odysseus' father Laertes, promising to choose one of the suitors when she completes the shroud. She sets up a loom in her room and begins to weave during the day, undoing her work at night. In this way, almost four years pass, until one of the serving women reveals her deception to the suitors, who force Penelope to complete the shroud.

It is at this point, following rumors of Odysseus' return, that a stranger arrives at the palace; it is Odysseus himself, disguised as a beggar. While conversing with the beggar, Penelope comes up with a new plan to choose the suitor who wins an archery contest, in which the stranger will also participate. The disguised Odysseus wins the contest, but Penelope seems unconvinced of his identity. She puts him to the test, asking for details regarding their marital bed that only he could know. Only after the stranger passes this test Penelope acknowledges him as her husband and the reunion is accomplished.

But until then, as noted above, Penelope mainly weeps. This extensive representation of her weeping is one of the elements that reinforce her image as an icon of absolute fidelity.[208] However, even female fidelity to a spouse is the central character trait that the storyteller wishes to commend, the story contains several twists relating to Penelope. Whether in a way that reflects or subverts the poet's intention, the epic shapes Penelope as a complex, enigmatic character; even her renowned fidelity comes under suspicion. Froma Zeitlin, for example, notes a contradiction between Penelope's description as a model of fidelity

---

208 According to Froma Zeitlin, Penelope's constant weeping in the work represents the constant presence of Odysseus in her consciousness, hence her absolute fidelity (Zeitlin 1996, 118–119).

and the accounts of several of her decisions that potentially could impede Odysseus' return.[209]

Others have wondered at the way several of Penelope's actions are described. Sheila Murnaghan writes that Penelope's character is hard to make sense of, and the things she says in the text cannot be understood at face value, especially in light of the weaving stratagem, which testifies to her cunning[210] Doherty finds especially puzzling Penelope's initiative in announcing the archery contest the victor of which she will wed. This move, which Penelope makes *after* being informed that Odysseus is fast approaching, triggered a polemic discourse among feminist readers who attribute her initiative to various contradictory motives.[211]

It is indeed challenging to reconcile the weeping, passive woman who lacks courage to act decisively with the woman whom the suitors' representative calls "sensible Penelope," a woman who has managed to restrain a pack of aggressive, unmannerly men for many years, and even to cunningly extract gifts from them (*Odyssey* 18.320 – 321). Out of the interpretative abundance concerning the riddle of Penelope, I will discuss three approaches that propose different directions for deciphering Penelope's enigmatic character, classified by the type of view each of them reflects: narrative view, feminist view, and quasi-legal view.

A narrative view is proposed by Bruce Louden. The Homeric storyteller, he argues, created a complex narrative template that is designed to lend prominence to Odysseus' cunning and resourcefulness in various ways, with the other characters being constructed to serve that purpose. This template also includes the repetitive theme of Odysseus' encounters with women who disguise their true motives, and Odysseus' success in deriving the most from these encounters despite the feminine insincerity.[212] According to this interpretation, then, the way the female characters are constructed – including Penelope, Nausicaa, and her mother Queen Arete – is harnessed by the epic storyteller to serve needs that relate primarily to the development of the character of the leading protagonist, Odysseus.

209 Zeitlin 1996, 118 – 119. For a description of various conceptions arising from Penelope's actions, especially in books XVIII – XIX, see Jonas Grethlein, "Homeric Motivation and Modern Narratology: The Case of Penelope," *The Cambridge Classical Journal* 64 (2018): 70 – 90.
210 Sheila Murnaghan, "Penelope's Agnoia: Knowledge, Power, and Gender in the Odyssey," in *Oxford Readings in Classical Studies: Homer's Odyssey*, ed. Lillian E. Doherty (Oxford: Oxford University Press, 2009), 231– 244, 232.
211 Doherty 1995, 15.
212 Bruce Louden, "An Extended Narrative Pattern in the Odyssey," *Greek, Roman and Byzantine Studies* 34. (1993): 5 – 33, 16 – 17.

An explanation of the riddle of Penelope based on a feminist view is proposed by Amy Kass and Adriana Cavarero, although the two proposals are almost opposed in their approach to understanding Penelope's mindset and motives. According to Kass, Penelope's central concern in life is to follow the instructions left her by her husband: to care for his parents and their son Telemachus, and to protect their house and property.[213] Her prolonged efforts to carry out these tasks and withstand the suitors' pressure to force her to abandon these instructions deplete her energy and cause Penelope to vacillate between bouts of activity and reclusive spells; they are the reason for the contradictions in her behavior.[214]

This reading posits at the forefront Penelope's responsibility as a wife and mother to ensure some degree of domestic and familial harmony despite the disruption caused by Odysseus' extended absence. To do so, Penelope, too, must undergo a process of losing her way and returning home herself. Due to weakness and desperation, she is not entirely focused on her goal of return, but at a certain stage she composes herself and her actions are those of faithful wife who aspires to a harmonious reunion with her husband.

Cavarero offers a different view, and identifies at the heart of Penelope's character not a commitment to the instructions left by her husband or an effort to defend the assets of the household, but a personal interest: Penelope is secretly fighting to retain the independence and unrestricted lifestyle she has enjoyed during her husband's prolonged absence. In this view, this desire is the central motive for her actions and decisions. Cavarero focuses on the most famous of Penelope's actions – the weaving and unraveling of the shroud, which lasted for several years. Penelope, she argues, uses a traditional women's handicraft – weaving – which is performed in her private rooms, not in order to highlight her faithfulness to Odysseus, but to create for herself a time and a space of her own where she undermines the existing order.[215]

A third, quasi-legal view is presented by Finley, who is puzzled by the suitors' willingness to wait for years without resorting to violence until Penelope chooses one of them. He puts the question as follows:

---

213 Amy Kass, "An Extended Narrative Pattern in the Odyssey," *Greek, Roman and Byzantine Studies* 34. (1993): 5–33 (Hebrew).

214 Kass describes the contradictions as follows: "She lets them wait in the bay, doesn't refuse their marriage offers but doesn't accept them either (1.249–250). She keeps her distance, but sends flattering messages (2.90–93; 13.381–380). She vacillates between active concern and passive reclusion. She weeps at night but is radiant by day" (My translation, Kass 2016).

215 Adriano Cavarero, *In Spite of Plato: A Feminist Rewriting of Ancient Philosophy* (Cambridge: Polity Press, 1995), 16.

[N]ot only did they publicly and repeatedly concede Telemachus' claim to his *oikos*, but they placed the decision in the strangest place imaginable, in the hands of a woman. There was nothing about the woman Penelope, either in beauty or wisdom or spirit, that justified this unprecedented and unwanted right of decision as a purely personal triumph. Institutionally, furthermore, this was a solidly patriarchal society, in which even a Telemachus could order his mother to leave the banquet hall and retire to her proper, womanly tasks.[216]

Although Finley suggests that Penelope's right of choice may represent the repressed memory of a primordial matriarchal regime that the author incorporated in the text,[217] he rejects this interpretation as farfetched and unfounded. He notes that neither Penelope nor Arete (to whom "masculine" powers were also attributed) was endowed with the genealogical lineage that could be traced to a matriarchal familial structure.[218] The alternative solution that Finley proposes to the riddle of Penelope ascribes quasi-legal motives to the suitors. Specifically, the suitors represent acknowledgment of Odysseus' family's right to the crown, of a principle that would come to be called "legitimacy" by kings of a later time. This principle, which echoes through the epics, is here reflected in the suitors' belief that Penelope's choice of one of their number might grant the new king "some shadow of legitimacy, however dim and fictitious."[219]

Each of the above approaches adds another thread to the complex web of Penelope's character. Let us begin with Louden's proposal to view Penelope's marginality and the paucity of references to her perspective as a poetic choice. In support of this view one might indeed point to the limited representation accorded to the "inner Penelope." Unlike Odysseus, whose interiority is accorded rich and multilayered representation, Penelope is described from a detached perspective. While the outer Penelope weeps, weaves, and undoes her weaving, the Homeric poet rarely lingers over the subtleties of her emotional states or the

---

216 Finley 1972, 87.

217 Susan Deacy, *Athena* (London: Routledge, 2008), 34–41. According to an approach that emerged at the beginning of the previous century, Greek mythology contains echoes of a matriarchal society in which women were dominant and whose ritual revolved around a "Great Goddess" who ruled nature and fertility. In the Bronze Age this society was replaced by a patriarchal society, centered on male dominion. On this view, Athena and other ancient goddesses are vestiges of the transition from matriarchy to patriarchy. Despite its considerable influence, this approach has been criticized by scholars who reject a connection between the frequency of female characters' appearances in the ancient writings and the conjectural existence of a period of matriarchal rule.

218 Finley 1972, 89.

219 Finley 1972, 89.

range of her inner reflections.[220] A close reading, however, reveals that the text alludes to what has been elided. In effect, by introducing us to a character in disguise, the storyteller is creating a constant tension between disclosure and concealment. For example, throughout the storyline Penelope exhibits external signs of faithfulness (such as her constant weeping and declarations of sorrow at Odysseus' absence), but she does not unequivocally refuse to marry another. Telemachus even complains, "She neither rejects a marriage she despises nor can she bear to bring the courting to an end" (*Odyssey* 1.290–291). According to Marilyn Katz, Penelope's inconsistent behavior is related to the strategies of disguise she employs to defend herself in the absence of her husband – the figure of authority whose duty it is to protect her.[221] According to this interpretation, to note the discrepancies and lack of consistency in Penelope's character does not constitute a reading contrary to the storyteller's intention; rather, the storyteller seems to be inviting us to spot them and ponder over their meaning. An example of such an inconsistency planted by the storyteller is when Athena, disguised as a stranger, tells Telemachus:

> As for your mother, if the spirit moves her to marry,
> let her go back to her father's house, a man of power.
> Her kin will arrange the wedding, provide the gifts [...] (*Odyssey* 1.316–318)

Ostensibly this remark belittles the importance of Penelope and her decisions, and at this stage it might be thought to reflect her secondary status in the narrative, in the spirit of Louden's approach. Later, however, behind the dismissive statement we find extensive engagement with Penelope and her motives, in which Athena is directly involved. Athena appears in Penelope's dreams and reassures her, plants the weaving stratagem in her mind, and in general tries to influence her conduct. In other words, the character of Athena, too, is harnessed by the storyteller to further refine the disguise that conceals Penelope's full consciousness.

Do Penelope's motives come across as a brave attempt to follow the instructions left her by her husband? The duplicity created by the narrative makes it difficult to answer the question definitively. On one hand, it is difficult not to notice Penelope's desire for independence and autonomy. She remains largely passive with respect to her husband's absence. She does not urge her son or others to set out in search of him; on the contrary, when Telemachus decides to embark on

---

220 Zeitlin 1996, 44.
221 Marilyn A. Katz, *Penelope's Renown: Meaning and Indeterminacy in the Odyssey* (Princeton, NJ: Princeton University Press, 2014), 193.

such a journey, she tries to delay his effort. In effect, Penelope's contribution to advancing Odysseus' homecoming is much less significant than the contributions of other women in the narrative. Against this background, and following Cavarero's interpretation, a secret desire to remain abandoned, as a means of retaining her independence, may go far toward explaining Penelope's conduct.

Another interpretation along these lines is suggested in Margaret Atwood's *The Penelopiad* (2005). Atwood rewrites the epic from Penelope's imagined viewpoint, attributing the rationale for the weaving stratagem to Penelope's desire to preserve her relative freedom and avoid becoming ensnared in a male net:

> The shroud itself became a story almost instantly. "Penelope's web", it was called; people used to say that of any task that remained mysteriously unfinished. I did not appreciate the term web. If the shroud was a web, then I was a spider. But I had not been attempting to catch men like flies: on the contrary, I'd merely been trying to avoid entanglement myself.[222]

However, reading Penelope's character as representing, first and foremost, a secretive striving toward freedom from male bonds obscures an important element. Although Penelope continuously postpones a decision, she never explicitly, or even by innuendo, dismisses the possibility of accepting one of the suitors. The Homeric storyteller even chooses to note that one of the suitors – Emphynomos, a well propertied prince – pleases her with his rhetoric skills: "Thanks to his timely words and good clear sense [...]" (*Odyssey* 16.442) The storyteller also elaborates on the economic interests at play, and Penelope's calculation whether it would be better to continue trying to preserve her existing property in Ithaca, which is slowly dwindling, or to choose a suitor that could provide her alternative economic resources. In conversation with a stranger (Odysseus in disguise) she explains her dilemma as follows:

> So my wavering heart goes shuttling, back and forth:
> Do I stay beside my son and keep all things secure –
> my lands, my serving-woman, the grand high-roofed house –
> true to my husband's bed, the people's voice as well?
> Or do I follow, at least the best man who courts me
> Here in the halls, who gives the greatest gifts? (*Odyssey* 19.591–596)

Penelope, then, has multifaceted considerations of her own that justify her lack of decisiveness and continuous postponements; fidelity is not necessarily fore-

---

222 Margaret Atwood, *The Penelopiad* (Edinburgh: Canongate, 2005), 119 (hereinafter abbreviated as Atwood, 2005).

most in her mind. There remains the puzzle noted by Finley with respect to her ability to maintain a lengthy status of indecision, and to put off the suitors, men of standing and power, for so long. Despite the pressure, Penelope manages to maintain this status for several years. One wonders at the source of her strength. But the answer suggested by Finley – that there was nothing unique about Penelope that justifies her right of decision, nor did she seek this autonomy of choice, and it was the suitors who chose to wait relatively patiently because they hoped to gain legitimacy for their own rule in Ithaca – is unconvincing. Finley's narrow conception of Penelope's character does not, however, accord with what the text places before us. What arises from the Homeric epic is the uniqueness of her personality. One of the suitors describes Penelope as follows:

> Quick to exploit the gifts Athena gave her –
> a skilled hand for elegant work, a fine mind
> and subtle wiles too – we've never heard the like [...]
> Not one could touch Penelope for intrigue (*Odyssey* 2.128–134)

Wilson, the first woman to translate the *Odyssey* into English, remarks:

> She's canny, she's strong-willed, she has grit, she has a vivid imagination, she's loyal, she's a competent, mostly single mother who shows deep love for her difficult, moody son, and she keeps a big and complex household running for two decades.[223]

Regarding the second part of his argument, it seems that ascribing to the suitors an understanding of subtleties relating to the laws of transfer of power is contrived, and, as Griffin notes, the suitors' behavior is related more closely to narrative needs than to any realpolitik considerations of the period.[224] Nonetheless, and perhaps dovetailing the quasi-legal direction that Finley proposes, Penelope's status in Ithaca, acquired by virtue of her marriage, is the source of a considerable degree of power and freedom of action, certainly in comparison to women in general. The king is absent, but the monarchical institution is strong enough to create an enclave inside which the queen conducts herself with relative freedom, and this occurs at a time when the bonds placed upon women were not yet so restrictive, as I elaborate below. Penelope stalls the suitors because she can do so: due both to the cultural and political circumstances in which her consent is crucial for the purpose of remarrying, and due to the force of her personality and personal skills.

---

223 Wilson, 2017.
224 See Griffin 2004, 84.

Of the approaches noted above, one attempts to decipher Penelope by identifying poetic intention, another by comparing what is told about her to what is known (or conjectured) about the historical period in which the epic was written, and a third reads her character from perspectives provided by feminist discourse. Reconciliation of these contradictory explanations of a fictional character's motives (or the conjectural intentions of its creator) is not practically possible, nor is there any need for it.[225] As is well known, part of the *Odyssey*'s lure lies in the breadth of interpretative fields it sparks. In that spirit, I propose to add a new dimension to the existing discourse concerning Penelope's character, one that potentially sheds new light on the contradictions and peculiarities of her character – the *Metis Syndrome.*

As outlined above, the female *Metis Syndrome* represents women's consciousness of the risks generated by an exposure of their full abilities, coupled with camouflaged efforts to retain the use of these abilities to influence their destiny. Atwood's description of Penelope's state of mind in *The Penelopiad* echoes the *Metis Syndrome.* Like many women, Atwood's Penelope finds it difficult to withstand the temptation to demonstrate her powers and agency: "Which of us can resist the temptation of being thought indispensable?"[226] At the same time, she holds back from doing so due to a residual memory of the fate that befell overly wise women in the ancient myths, and pragmatically concludes that a woman had best not demonstrate excessive cunning or sagacity, especially not to her spouse: "Cleverness is a quality a man likes to have in his wife as long as she is some distance away from him."[227]

What does Penelope's heart truly crave in the course of the prolonged singlehood that she found herself in? Athena raises the question, yet the text offers no unequivocal answer. Homer tells us little about Penelope's inner thoughts, instead describing her conduct in some detail, inviting his audience to notice the discrepancies and the contradictions.

Penelope's inconsistent decisions to remain silent or speak on different occasions represent the choices available to women within the inherent trade-off signified by the female *Metis Syndrome.* On two occasions Telemachus silences his mother and commands her to leave the public rooms and retire to her private quarters. On the first occasion, in Book I, Penelope asks the bard Phemius to cease reciting a song describing the Trojan War because of the sorrow the

---

225 For more on the nature of the interpretive ascription of motives to fictional characters, see Robert W. Reiber, *Freud on Interpretation: The Ancient Magical Egyptian and Jewish Traditions* (New York: Springer, 2012), 50–51.
226 Atwood 2005, 80.
227 Atwood 2005, 29.

words cause her. Telemachus defends Phemius' poetic freedom to recite "Any way the spirit stirs him on" (*Odyssey* 1.309) and commands his mother: "Go back to your quarters [...] I hold the reins of power in this house" (*Odyssey* 1.410 – 414). Penelope chooses to comply and withdraw. On the second occasion, in Book XX, Penelope debates with her suitor Eurymachus whether the stranger – the disguised Odysseus – is entitled to participate in the archery contest she has arranged. Telemachus intervenes in the discussion, again ordering his mother to leave:

> So, mother
> Go back to your quarters, Tend to your own tasks [...]
> I hold the reins of power in this house. (*Odyssey* 21.390 – 395).

Once again Penelope withdraws.

In an essay on the historical roots and contemporary manifestations of silencing women's public voice, Mary Beard describes the silencing of Penelope in Book I as "the first recorded example of a man telling a woman to 'shut up'" in Western literature,[228] exemplifying the way in which the practice of silencing of women signified men's maturation.[229] Beard links the practice of silencing women in the ancient world and gender inequality in subsequent historical periods, including denial of the right to vote, diminution of their legal and economic status, and the systematic weakening of women's agency, which continues in various ways to this day. According to Beard, the rectification of this situation requires the deconstruction of this template, which has been imprinted upon us by the classical narratives, and initially so by the *Odyssey*. Beard writes: "We need to work that out before we figure out how we modern Penelopes might answer back to our own Telemachuses [...]"[230]

Appropriate as it to join such call, I would argue that Penelope does not exclusively represent the humiliation of being silenced, diminished and excluded, but also the female power of resistance. Both occasions on which Telemachus silenced her and Penelope withdrew are described similarly. The first time "She took to heart/ the clear good sense in what her son had said" (*Odyssey* 1.416 – 417) and the second time too "She took to heart/ the clear good sense in what her son had said" (*Odyssey* 21.397). The result is a modular repetition that reflects the male aspect of the *Metis Syndrome*. At the same time, the epic

---

228 Mary Beard, "The Public Voice of Women," *Women's History Review* 24.5 (2015): 809 – 818, 809 (hereinafter abbreviated as: Beard 2015).
229 Beard 2015, 818.
230 Beard 2015, 818.

itself undermines this androcentric viewpoint, giving expression to female power by reflecting the female *Metis Syndrome,* the constant trade-off between a desire to maintain agency and an awareness of its risks.

Beard focuses on a single episode, yet the narrative in entirety reveals that Penelope's acquiescence to her son's command (which is indeed rather absurd, as Beard rightly notes, in light of Telemachus' young age and inexperience versus his mother's impressive character and experience) does not represent her typical conduct and her expert navigation between the private and public sphere. In other episodes, Penelope chooses to speak in public, and when she does so her voice is adamant and has an immediate effect on the proceedings. The same Penelope that at a certain moment decides to retire to her quarters decides at another moment to appear in the public space, confront the suitors directly, and openly denounce their behavior:

> Listen to me, my overbearing friends!
> You who plague this palace night and day,
> Drinking, eating us out of house and home
> With the lord and master absent, gone so long –
> The only excuse that you can offer is your zest
> To win me as your bride (*Odyssey* 21.70 – 73)

Here, Penelope offers one of the first examples in Western literature of a strong, assertive female response, capable of rebuffing men whose actions would likely be categorized today as sexual harassment. Not only does she rebuff them, she manages to manipulate her male adversaries into agreeing to the archery contest that she cool-headedly plans on the basis of an intuition regarding the stranger's true identity. Only after ascertaining that the contest will take place and that the stranger will participate does she heed her son's command (which, once again, is presented as a somewhat ridiculous demand) and exits the public space.

Even away from the public eye, in the privacy between herself and her spouse, Penelope evinces no less resolution, deciding to test the man she believes to be Odysseus, though she is not entirely certain. Their marital bed is built around a tree trunk and is immovable, but Penelope tells the stranger a blatant lie about the bed having been moved, to test his reaction. Odysseus passes the test, bursting into a rage, but after the fit of joyous weeping that is expected of her, Penelope calmly explains to him the reason for her excessive caution:

> In my heart of hearts I always cringed with fear
> Some fraud might come, beguile
> me with his talk;

The world is full of the sort,
Cunning ones who plot their own dark ends (*Odyssey* 23.242–245)

The lesson taught by the ancient story of Metis, for whom Zeus set a rhetorical trap that enabled him to swallow her, is the always-present backdrop to Penelope's excessive caution. Metis was swallowed because she did not suspect her spouse; Penelope prefers to be suspicious and despite her son's remonstrations (who ironically accuses her of being overly cruel: "Oh mother [...] cruel mother, you with your hard heart!" see *Odyssey* 23.111–112) and the fury of the man who soon will be identified with certainty as her husband, she will not let down her guard before she receives assurances of his identity and her own future status. The *Metis Syndrome* clarifies Penelope's vicissitudes of character; she is a woman who weeps in public at every opportunity, but behind the veil of tears, she is constantly scheming and influencing the course of events to her advantage. The *Metis Syndrome* elucidates why, on many occasions, Penelope chooses to disguise her cunning and resourcefulness and conceal her true abilities. The weeping, the weaving, the obedient retirement to her quarters – these are all masks that Penelope dons to protect herself and retain her relative freedom of action.

Acknowledgment of the *Metis Syndrome* meshes with an unsentimental reading of the character, as proposed by Wilson.[231] Such a reading would consider that Odysseus always has choices, many of which he exercises in the course of the epic. He travels freely, disguises himself, tells falsehoods, exchanges identities to protect his interests, and meets a remarkable array of men, women, and goddesses, including two with whom he has sexual relations. Penelope's free will space, on the other hand, is much more restricted. She can only choose between her status as wife of Odysseus and her status as the wife of another man, and even that choice is available for only a limited time (*Odyssey* 23.111–112). Within these constraints, Penelope operates with utmost effectiveness to influence her future. The *Metis Syndrome* clarifies how she goes about it.

231 Wilson, 2017.

Calypso and Circe

Calypso and Circe are both half-Titans by birth.[232] Their encounters with Odysseus mirror the inherent tension between the divine and the human and between male and female.[233] Their portrayal by the Homeric storyteller also reverberates the myth of Metis.

I will begin with Calypso. On the seven years during which Odysseus was her bedmate, Homer provides the viewpoints of both Calypso and Odysseus. Odysseus speaks of Calypso in his conversation with Arete, queen of the Phaeacians, who wishes to hear about his travels. Odysseus frames his relationship with Calypso as having been decreed by the gods:

> [...] Drifted along nine days. On the tenth, at dead of night,
> The gods cast me up on Ogygia, Calypso's island (*Odyssey* 7.291–292)

Although he does mention Calypso's grace and affection, Odysseus mainly describes her unsuccessful efforts to tempt him to stay with her by promising him immortality.

Calypso has a different perspective, which we learn from her conversation with Hermes, the god who was dispatched from Olympus to instruct her to send Odysseus on his way. At the center of her story is neither a divine decree nor a failed seduction but rather her own personal decision to engage in an act of rescue, and then to share her life with the rescued man:

> The man I saved,
> Riding astride his keel-board, all alone, when Zeus
> With one hurl of a white-hot bolt had crushed
> His racing warship down [...] (*Odyssey* 5.144–147)

Calypso's story is comprised of a series of independent choices, made willingly and out of love: She chooses to save Odysseus' life, and then to live with him as her partner, and offer him eternal youth and immortality if he remains with her. She considers the gods' denial of the opportunity to establish a permanent relationship with Odysseus as a denial of her rights, which should be granted to her

---

232 Calypso is the daughter of the Titan Atlas and the nymph Pleione (see *Odyssey* at 461). Circe is the daughter of Helios, the sun god, and the nymph Perse (see *Odyssey* at 191). In both cases the father is a Titan, the mother a nymph, making both half-Titans by birth.
233 Stehle 1996, 202.

just as they are granted to the male gods. She ascribes this denial of rights to her and other goddesses[234] to the male gods' envy and double standards:

> Hard-hearted
> You are, you gods! You unrivalled lords of jealousy –
> Scandalized when goddesses sleep with mortals,
> Openly, when even one has made the man her husband (*Odyssey* 5.130 – 133)

Calypso's complaint in effect points to the structural inequality between male and female, reflected, for example, in the absolute sexual freedom that men – gods and mortals alike – claim for themselves, as opposed to the restrictions on the sexual freedom of women, both goddesses and mortals. Penelope, the leading female protagonist in the *Odyssey*, is revered as a role model due to her sexual fidelity; Clytemnestra's adultery justifies her murder; the serving women pay with their lives for their suspected sexual infidelity to the House of Odysseus. Odysseus, in contrast, does not appear to be burdened by a duty of sexual fidelity to Penelope. He reiterates his longing for his wife even as he chooses to engage in sexual relations with Calypso and with Circe. The passing references to his sexual infidelity are devoid of any judgmental overtones. Calypso embodies the resulting discordance, which is especially striking considering the Homeric storyteller's repeated praise of Penelope's fidelity.[235] From her enclaved habitat, Calypso demands a law of equality for male and female.

The retort she receives from Hermes, the emissary of the gods, utterly disregards Calypso's principled argument. Rather, Hermes refers to power in a way that speaks to the memory of Metis' fate, and reminds the half-Titaness seeking to break out of her constraints that Zeus the all-might god must not be crossed.

Eva Stehle explains why Calypso's failure is inevitable against the background of the ancient narratives' unequivocal inclination to eliminate any evidence of female superiority, even in the case of an immortal woman versus a mortal man, as in the case of Odysseus and Calypso:

> If the divine/human hierarchy is emphasized at the expense of the male/female one, an autonomous, sexually active female figure, one who controls the phallus, is created.

---

234 Calypso is referring to other cases in which the gods reacted with violence to goddesses' choice of mortal men. One such is the choice by Eos, Goddess of Dawn, of Orion, a mortal hunter who paid for it with his life. Another is the story of Demeter, Goddess of Corn and sister of Zeus, who lay with Iasion, a mortal warrior, who was smitten by the gods (*Odyssey* 5.119 – 120).
235 For the double standard described by Calypso, see John Peradotto, *Man in the Middle Voice: Name and Narration in the Odyssey* (Princeton, NJ: Princeton University Press, 1990, 54 – 56.

Thus, cultural logic, through this myth pattern, can potentially offer narratives that subvert male dominance. In fact, public narratives from early Greece avoid this outcome.[236]

Although the *Odyssey* allows Calypso to present her case at length, to put forward her arguments, and make a show of strength, Calypso has no chance against Zeus, who is ordering her to relinquish Odysseus.[237] Like Metis before her, who, according to myth, chose to assist Zeus and continues to offer him her sage counsel even after his abuse, Calypso accepts the structural gender inequality that limits her options of action, and generously applies her full abilities to help Odysseus continue on his journey.

Calypso repeatedly emphasizes her intention of helping Odysseus return home, yet Odysseus, under the spell of the *Metis Syndrome*, is suspicious of Calypso's motives and forces her to swear that she will not harm him. She answers graciously:

> All I have in mind and devise for you
> are the very plans I'd fashion for myself,
> If I were in your straits (*Odyssey* 5.208 – 210)

According to Maja Pellikaan-Engel's analysis, Calypso turns into an ethical role model: She turns out to be a compassionate, intelligent woman with a highly developed moral sense, rather than the egoistic seductress she is commonly considered to be. Calypso's condemnation of the double standard and her view that rationality and empathy together form the basis of proper moral conduct sound surprisingly modern.[238]

Unlike Calypso, Circe is given no opportunity to tell her version of the story in the Homeric text. Odysseus' description of Circe is puzzling. He frames their encounter as his confrontation with an "awesome power" (*Odyssey* 10.149) that has an evil brother, a personage who'd been "murderous-minded" (*Odyssey* 10.151) toward him, trying to ensnare him with her "witch's subtle craft" (*Odyssey* 10.320). Odysseus somehow survives this threat with the help of a protective drug and his sword:

> The moment Circe strikes with her long thin wand,
> You draw your sharp sword sheathed at your hip
> And rush her fast as if to run her through! (*Odyssey* 10.325 – 327)

---

236 Stehle 1996, 203.
237 Stehle 1996, 204.
238 From her lecture on the topic, Maja Pellikaan-Engel, "Calypso's Recipe: On Biased Traditions in Philosophy," *Western Libraries* (website) June 26, 2010.

Lo and behold, that selfsame incredibly evil and mighty goddess-nymph is instantaneously subdued by a mere mortal. The terrified Circe, Odysseus tells the Phaeacian queen and the fascinated audience in the palace, screamed, fell to her knees, and offered him sex. In 2018, Madeline Miller published a novel centered on the character of Circe in which she describes the internal contradiction that arises from Odysseus' report:

> Circe was a goddess, why was she afraid of the sword? ... Odysseus shows a blade, and suddenly she has to kneel and offer herself to him?[239]

The *Metis Syndrome* may offer an answer to this puzzle and to Odysseus' story of his encounter with Circe. The Homeric storyteller portrays their encounter from the male perspective that views women and femininity as a constant threat that can be lifted only through a collocation of cunning and brute force. In other words, Circe signifies female power that is a threat to be subdued and a source of advantage that requires exploitation.[240] As Miller puts it,

> A woman who could control men was unacceptable. She must be corrected by the hero, set back in her place. Instead of Odysseus being transformed by her spell, she is the one changed: from potent, independent goddess to bedmate, helpmeet, and patient nurse of men's pain.[241]

According to Stehle, the Odysseus-Circe episode is related to a common narrative template in mythology, in which the gods are recruited to neutralize female power whenever it threatens male interests. When Circe becomes a threat to his planned homecoming, Odysseus enjoys the protection of the gods, who neutralize her power:

> By neutralizing Kirke's power, the gods arrange it so that the male/female hierarchy will predominate from the start and Kirke accommodate herself to Odysseus [242]

---

239 From a talk by author Madeline Miller on her novel dealing with Circe's character, expanding on the subject, see Madeline Miller, "Restoring Power to The Women of Ancient Myth," *Literary Hub* (website) April 11, 2018b 2018b. (hereinafter abbreviated as Miller 2018b) For the novel itself, see Madeline Miller, *Circe* (New York, NY: Little, Brown and Company, 2018a).

240 For a view of Circe as representing the essential characterization of women in the *Odyssey*, see Charles Segal, "Circean Temptations: Homer, Vergil, Ovid," *Transactions and Proceedings of the American Philological Association* 99 (1968): 419–442, 419.

241 Miller 2018b.

242 Stehle 1996, 204.

Through Circe, then, the *Odyssey* gives expression to men's fear of female power – the male aspect of the *Metis Syndrome.* While the narrative centers on male success in overcoming the female threat, the *Odyssey* leaves space for female generosity, empathy, and traits associated with the feminine. As the story progresses, Circe's menace is written out of the myth, making room for an exhibition of her striking magnanimity and even warmth toward Odysseus and his men. She returns Odysseus' men, whom she had turned to swine, to human form, not only unharmed but also taller and handsomer than ever. She provides an abundance of meat and red wine for the entire company for an entire year, and to Odysseus himself she also grants the pleasures of her bed. When he decides to leave, Circe gives him lifesaving navigational guidance and instructions for the course that lies ahead of him. Indeed, from the account of their encounter, Circe emerges as ominous, yet also as having a generous, even loving nature, and also as the source of wise counsel to Odysseus that was indispensable for his return home.[243]

In subsequent generations what would come to be emphasized are the menacing aspects of the two women, Calypso and Circe. Over time, Circe was increasingly identified as a cruel, fearsome sorceress, and the aspect of her generosity faded.[244] Calypso's image as a sexual predator became transfixed in literature and culture.[245] Both women became cultural stereotypes of threatening female desire.

In summary, like their primordial foremother Metis, both Calypso and Circe are women of extraordinary power. The myth places their ability to provide wise counsel and solve problems at the service of men. Their characters feature a combination of practical cunning and generosity, sensitivity, and altruism. And like Metis, they too pay a price for overstepping the boundaries of their allotted agency. For her attempt to exercise her power and agency, the primordial Titaness is swallowed and imprisoned in Zeus' body. Both Circe and Calypso are

---

243 Cedric Hubbell Whitman, *Homer and the Heroic Tradition* (Cambridge, MA: Harvard University Press, 1958), 300. Cedric Whitman describes how Circe starts out in the narrative as an evil witch and ends as the Good Fairy.

244 Judit Gera, "The Voice of Circe," in *das rechte Maß getroffen*, eds. Ernő Kulcsár Szabó, Károly Manherz and Magdolna Orosz (Budapest: Eötvös-Loránd Universität, 2004), 215 – 223, 215. Judit Gera describes the development as follows: "In later stories, however, Circe has become a frightening and cruel sorceress. Instead, of the harmony and balance of the human values of men and women in Homer's work, there came polarization. Circe has become the inscrutable, ferocious female, the Other, the enemy of men. Somebody who causes anxiety and chaos."

245 Jenifer Neils, "Les Femmes Fatales: Skylla and the Sirens in Greek Art," in *The Distaff Side: Representing the Female in Homer's Odyssey*, ed. Beth Cohen (New York: Oxford University Press, 1995), 175 – 184, 175.

sequestered on a remote island, sentenced to isolation that prevents them from forging bonds of solidarity or mutual assistance with other women. Nonetheless, they both manage to make their voices heard and their presence felt, to act and influence. In fact, their isolation charges their characters with special power, for it underscores their ability to live outside patriarchal domination and not in subservience to it. Moreover, both genuinely choose to help Odysseus, and without their assistance he would never have returned to Ithaca.

Nausicaa and Arete

Almost a quarter of the *Odyssey* is devoted to Odysseus' stay in Scheria, the kingdom of the Phaeacians. After hosting Odysseus generously, the Phaeacians load a fast ship with gifts and propel Odysseus back to his homeland. Odysseus owes the improvement in his situation to the active efforts of two women: Arete, queen of the Phaeacians and her daughter, the princess Nausicaa. Due to the choices and actions of these two women, Odysseus benefits from the Phaeacians' assistance.

The Phaeacian episode celebrates female power, and some have even identified elements of gender reversal in Phaeacian society with respect to social custom and norms in the times of which the Homeric epic speaks.[246] Nonetheless, there are several puzzling aspects to the episodes involving Nausicaa and Arete.

I will begin with Nausicaa, the daughter of King Alcinous and Queen Arete. The Homeric storyteller emphasizes her young age, innocence, and timidity, yet identifies her as a threat to Odysseus[247] and a menacing seductress.[248] In a famous essay that details women's central role in the *Odyssey*, nineteenth-century writer Samuel Butler describes the princess as an assertive character whose will must not be opposed:

---

246 H. A. Shapiro, "Coming of Age in Phaiakia: The Meeting of Odysseus and Nausicaa," in *The Distaff Side: Representing the Female in Homer's Odyssey*, ed. Beth Cohen (New York: Oxford University Press, 1995), 155–164, 155.
247 For more on Nausicaa as representing a threat to Odysseus, see Micholas P. Gross, "Nausicaa: A Feminine Threat," *The Classical World* 69.5 (1976): 311–317, 316 (hereinafter abbreviated as: Gross 1976); Nancy Felson Robin, *Regarding Penelope: From Character to Poetics* (Princeton, NJ: Princeton University Press, 1994), 46. In the spirit of this position, Nausicaa too, like other female characters remindful of her such as Circe and Calypso, has the potential to cause damage. See Doherty 1995, 85.
248 According to such a view, Nausicaa in her self-restrained fashion tries to seduce Odysseus. See Charles Rowan Beye, *The Iliad, the Odyssey, and the Epic Tradition* (Garden City, NY: Doubleday, 1996), 196.

> Take Nausicaa again, delightful as she is, it would not be wise to contradict her; she knows what is good for Ulysses, and all will go well with him so long as he obeys her, but she must be master and he man.[249]

Turning to Arete, it has frequently been noted that the way in which Nausicaa and Athena refer to her power gives rise to unfulfilled expectations, and that in effect the queen is not as central or significant a figure as she might initially seem.[250] The Phaeacian queen and her daughter are described somewhat ambiguously: They are powerful and cunning yet cautious and averse to attention. Viewing them through the prism of the *Metis Syndrome* may resolve these discrepancies and turn both Arete and Nausicaa into fuller, better understood characters.

As Nausicaa and her handmaidens play on the beach, a missed ball rolls into the current. The girls' cries arouse Odysseus from his slumber. With only a few leaves and encrusted sea salt hiding his nakedness, he emerges from the shelter of the forest. Nausicaa's handmaidens flee in terror, but she remains calm and listens to what the "sly and suave" (*Odyssey* 6.162) stranger has to say. He first expresses his astonishment at Nausicaa's beauty and her resemblance to the goddess Artemis, then goes on to describe his misfortune and asks for help. He concludes by wishing her a salutary conjugality to be granted by the gods. Showing self-confidence and control of the situation, Nausicaa calms her handmaidens as Odysseus sees to bettering his looks. Athena adds a touch of her own by imbuing him with special grace. Nausicaa gazes at the radiant stranger and starts thinking about a possible future with this man, a theme the stranger has injected into the conversation.

From the outset, then, their encounter is framed by potential wedlock. It is Athena in disguise that plants in the princess's mind the idea of preparing her wardrobe for marriage. Though Nausicaa is too embarrassed to speak to her father directly about "her hopes for marriage" (*Odyssey* 6.75), the king is sensitive enough to infer her wishes, and he helps to put her plan into action. Against this backdrop, together with Odysseus' praise of harmonious conjugality – even as he carefully avoids mentioning the fact that he himself has long since found such – it is almost inevitable that Nausicaa should conclude that only the gods could

---

249 Samuel Butler, *The Authoress of the Odyssey* (London: Longmans, Green, 1897), 107.
250 Helene Whittaker, "The Status of Arete in the Phaeacian Episode of the Odyssey," *Symbolae Osloenses* 74.1 (1999/2008): 140–50, 140; Marios Skempis and Ioannis Ziogas, "Arete's Words: Etymology, Ehoie-Poetry and Gendered Narrative in the Odyssey," in *Narratology and Interpretation*, eds. Jonas Grethlein and Antonios Rengakos (Berlin: De Gruyter, 2009), 213–240, 240.

have contrived her encounter with the stranger, in response to her secret wish: "Ah, if only a man like *that* were called my husband!" (*Odyssey* 6.270).

From this point on, Nausicaa takes action to further what the reader recognizes as unattainable: transforming the stranger into a legitimate candidate for marriage. At a later stage – much later than would have been appropriate – and only after the king almost explicitly proposes that Odysseus marries his daughter, Odysseus reveals his identity and married status. However, the important point in this story is not the late stage at which Odysseus makes his disclosure, but the power and the resourcefulness of the young princess: even before this disclosure, Nausicaa manages to transform the anonymous stranger who has been cast up on the seashore into a respected figure in the royal court.

Nausicaa carefully plans the stranger's entry into the city, explaining the relevant norms and what they entail. She is aware of the rules of conduct that apply to girls and young women, including those that forbids meetings with men before marriage,[251] and equally aware that openly flaunting this rule would tarnish her reputation. Still, she chooses to do exactly what the rules forbid: She conducts significant communications with an anonymous stranger and plans another meeting with him. At the same time she offers him guidance as to how to elicit the community's favor and sympathy toward him. She instructs him to enter the city alone, find the palace, and first seek out her mother, Queen Arete, on whose decision, she informs him, his fate rests.

Odysseus follows the careful directions he is given. Again, King Alcinous manages to guess his daughter's will even when she does not explicitly express it. Considering the mysterious stranger's anonymity and the availability of Phaeacian bidders for her hand in marriage, it is surprising that the king declares the stranger to be a possible groom for his daughter. When it emerges that no such marriage is possible, and Odysseus leaves to return to his wife and home, Nausicaa expresses no explicit disappointment though she devotes her final words to remind him that he will ever be beholden to her:

> Farewell, my friend! And when you are at home,
> Home in your own land, remember me at times.
> Mainly to me you owe the gift of life (*Odyssey* 8.518 – 520)

Odysseus concedes the existence of the debt: "You saved my life, dear girl" (*Odyssey* 8.526). However, he keeps the memories to himself and when he tells Penelope about his wanderings after his return to Ithaca, he makes no mention of the girl who saved his life.

---

251 Gross 1976, 313.

Nausicaa understands she is required to conform to strict rules and norms. The need for caution when circumventing these rules is branded into her as it is into all women. She knows that her status does not exempt her from compliance with norms of sexual modesty and subservience to male dominance. Despite her young age and inexperience, she takes control of her life and enjoys autonomy through caution and cleverness. The feasibility of such control open to women in the period of the epics is further supported by Queen Arete's character.

Arete's name first arises when Nausicaa gives Odysseus detailed instructions regarding his subsequent conduct. Everything depends on your finding favor in the queen's eyes, Nausicaa tells him. She instructs him to arrive at the palace, walk past her father, the king, and kneel at the queen's knees. Before describing the encounter, Homer uses Athena's remarks to Odysseus to provide additional information about the queen: She is a woman who is held in great esteem by her husband and by the people, due to her common sense and her mediating skills that allow her to resolve disputes among men.

Odysseus follows Nausicaa's instructions. He arrives at the palace, throws his arms around Arete's knees, and entreats her to help him return to his home. The queen remains silent. Upon the advice of the elderly nobleman Echeneus, to whom we shall have occasion to return, King Alcinous raises Odysseus from the earth and orders a sumptuous banquet for him.

This is a charged scene. Acting on Nausicaa's advice, Odysseus produces a visual representation of the queen's power and authority: He kneels at her feet in a public act that underscores his awareness of her power. Echeneus breaks up this scene, shunts aside the queen's supreme status and ushers in a different symbolism that represents the king's authority.

During the banquet and afterwards, the queen remains silent. Arete addresses Odysseus only after all the attendees have left the hall, when the serving women are clearing the tables. The timing is not coincidental, as the questions she asks are of a sensitive nature. Because they concern Nausicaa's conduct it is only natural for Arete, calculating by nature, to prefer to ascertain the answers to these questions without an audience. Arete asks the stranger direct questions, striking in their contrast to the flowery rhetoric and pleasantries voiced until now by the men. Her first question is:

> Stranger,
> I'll be the first to question you – myself.
> Who are you? Where are you from? (*Odyssey* 7.272–275)

Her second question concerns the contradiction between his stories of a journey at sea and the fact that the clothes Odysseus is wearing, which Arete recognizes, belong to Nausicaa:

> Who gave you the clothes you're wearing now?
> Didn't you say you reached us roving on the sea? (*Odyssey* 7.275–276)

Odysseus avoids answering the second question, answering the first at length. The clothes he is wearing were given him by Nausicaa, he says, adding that the princess treated him with faultless courtesy and intelligence. At this stage, Arete already knows several things: that the princess's reputation may be at risk due to her unusual dealings with the stranger, and that Nausicaa has a special interest in him. Arete remains silent. The king's response underscores the stringent rules of conduct to which all women are subject. Nausicaa has flaunted custom, he notes. She should have brought the guest to the palace together with her attendants, and not taken leave of him after their meeting. In reply, Odysseus lies to protect the princess's reputation and his own: It was he himself, he says, who decided, for reasons of modesty and apprehension, to appear at the palace alone. The explanation satisfies the king who finds the stranger so much to his liking that he proposes to Odysseus that he remain in the kingdom as his prospective son-in-law:

> If only
> Seeing the man you are, seeing we think as one
> *You* could wed my daughter and be my son-in-law
> And stay right here with us. I'd give you a house
> And great wealth – if you chose to stay (*Odyssey* 7.357–360)

Arete still does not say a word, and Odysseus refrains from revealing his true identity and his married status. The next day he arrives at the assembly of the Phaeacians, in the course of which games are held, and singing and dancing, and gifts of friendship are showered upon him. The second time Arete speaks to Odysseus is in reference to something seemingly trivial. She advises him to carefully guard the lid of the chest of gifts she gave him at the king's instructions, but she calls him "stranger," in a way that alludes to the mystery surrounding his identity, and that her second question was never answered. Perhaps in connection to the queen's implied demand for additional information, the king asks the stranger to identify himself by name. Odysseus finally concedes and recounts at length about his wanderings since leaving Troy. Toward the end of the story, he describes his meeting in Hades with all the wives and daughters of the heroes. Everyone is hushed, enthralled by the dark story, except for

Arete. For the first time, perhaps because of a growing certainty that Odysseus must be under the protection of Olympus, she affirms his status as her personal guest, concurrently declaring that all the Phaeacians must show him respect and generously offer him gifts.

As it initially unfolds, this scene confirms the queen's power and authority, which is, again, undermined by the elderly Echeneus. He concurs with the queen's orders, saying that all the assembly members accept them, and that they should be obeyed. But he adds:

> [...] Though on Alcinous here
> Depend all words and action (*Odyssey* 11.393–394)

Echeneus, says Helene Whittaker, is in effect subtly reprimanding the queen for her improper demonstration of authority.[252] The king responds to Echeneus' remarks and confirms the queen's declaration by virtue of his own authority.[253] The brief scene is colored by tension between the autonomous authority the queen seeks and what patriarchal society permits her. [254]

Finley finds the references to Arete's power "strange" in view of the many explicit demonstrations of monarchical authority exercised by her husband, King Alcinous.[255] He discusses two types of explanations. First, he rejects the view that the contradictions in Arete's character reflect contradictory traditions associated with the Phaeacians that were subsumed into the *Odyssey*.[256] He then offers a poetic explanation: Scheria, which is characterized in the *Odyssey* as a place located between the real and the fantastical, represents a stage in Odysseus' transition from the domain of the supernatural, where his relations have been with goddesses, monsters, and Cyclopes, to earthly Ithaca. According to this interpretation, the manifestations of female power belong to the fantastical dimension that Odysseus is leaving behind as he approaches Ithaca.[257]

This interpretation is doubtful. The explicit and implied references to female power in the *Odyssey* are not concentrated in the realm of the fantastical. Mentions of the power, resourcefulness, and vigorous action by women constitute a significant part of the *Odyssey*'s storyline. The epic tells of a world in which

---

252 Helene Whittaker, "The Status of Arete in the Phaeacian Episode of the Odyssey," *Symbolae Osloenses* 74.1 (1999/2008): 140–50, 141.

253 Michael N. Nagler, "Penelope's Male Hand: Gender and Violence in the Odyssey," *Colby Quarterly* 29.3 (1993): 241–257, 249 (hereinafter abbreviated as: Nagler 1993).

254 On the various contradictions in her character, see Nagler 1993, 242.

255 Finley 1972, 88.

256 Finley 1972, 88

257 Finley 1972, 87.

women of different classes – immortals and mortals, noblewomen and serving women – have the agency to influence their own destinies and those of men. Most of them do so cautiously and in a calculated fashion. So too in Scheria: Arete and Nausicaa vacillate between concealing their power and trying to exercise it; between the need to demonstrate compliance with the androcentric rules and norms and their willingness to assume risks to protect and promote their personal interests. Scheria allows this duality to exist, and it is given expression through the contradictions in the characters of the mother and daughter. Both are "permitted" to express their will and exercise power, even as they try – are even committed to – drawing as little attention as possible to their agency. Like Metis, any woman who disrupts this delicate balance is liable to pay a heavy price.

This kind of fluidity may be especially prominent in Scheria, for it emerges that the Phaeacians had been flouting a specific divine decree for decades. When Alcinous comprehends the nature of the assistance that Odysseus is requesting, he is reminded that he had heard from his father that Poseidon, God of the Ocean, had forbidden the Phaeacians from granting safe passage to strangers, or otherwise be punished. Notwithstanding, Alcinous disregards this order, commanding that Odysseus be conveyed back to his homeland on a Phaeacian ship. Angry Poseidon is given permission by Zeus to punish the Phaeacians, and turns the ship to stone upon its return to the city after Odysseus' disembarkation in Ithaca. In the face of an impending catastrophe of having Poseidon drop a mountain on their city, Alcinous declares the start of a new era, an era of full abidance by the norm that until now has been ignored:

> Hurry, friends, do as I say, let us all comply:
> Stop our convoys home for every castaway
> chancing on our city! (*Odyssey* 13.203 – 205)

Even if Scheria is saved, the new era puts an end to the fluidity that afforded the women of Scheria and the women in the world of the Homeric epics a certain degree control over the course of their lives. The emergent rule of law will increasingly expose them to men's policing gaze.

The Serving Women

Serving women, housekeepers, and maids turn up often throughout the *Odyssey*. In the Phaeacian palace, in Odysseus' palace, and in the palace of Menelaus and

Helen, they care for children, do laundry, clean, cook, grind flour, weave, anoint men with oil, make beds and prepare baths.[258]

There were 50 women serving in Odysseus' household, the storyteller informs us (*Odyssey* 22.421).[259] Maids first appear in the *Odyssey* when Penelope makes her initial appearance. The queen carefully choreographs the scene: she walks down the grand staircase, stopping beside a pillar that supports the beam of the roof, grasping a luminous scarf, with a waiting-woman on either side of her (*Odyssey* 1.335). Several times in the course of the story she devises an identical *tableau vivant*, in which the waiting-women – who are always called "devoted" – serve as props employed to create a specific picture and atmosphere for the suitors.

As the story progresses, several serving women are given a name,[260] and two even play a certain part in the storyline: Eurycleia, the elderly nurse of Odysseus and his son Telemachus, and young Melantho, whom Penelope is grooming.

The unfolding story of these two characters conveys a clear message: good serving women exhibit unquestioning loyalty to the household and its masters. Their reward is being allowed to continue living and serving the household, while disloyal serving women will pay with their lives. Eurycleia and Melantho are the two faces of the good servant/bad servant dichotomy.[261] Tracing the deeper layers of this dichotomy, however, reveals another manifestation of the *Metis Syndrome*: men's suspicions and fear of women – including women servants –

---

258 According to Finley 1992, 53, most of the slaves in the household described in the epics are women who were captured as spoils of war. The victors typically killed the remaining enemy men, or released them for ransom, and captured the women, who were forced to share their masters' beds in many cases.

259 There are male slaves in the household as well, like the swineherd Eumaeus, a nobleman who was kidnapped and sold into slavery, and Melanthius, Melantho's brother, a servant whose disloyalty to the House of Odysseus is punished by a brutal death. The differences between the respective representations of male and female servants/slaves in the *Odyssey* are discussed by William G. Thalmann, "Female Slaves in the Odyssey," in *Women and Slaves in Greco-Roman Culture*, eds. Sandra R. Joshel and Sheila Murnaghan (London: Routledge, 1998), 22–34, 28–29 (hereinafter abbreviated s Thalmann 1998). Thalmann notes that even though all slaves and servants in the epic are to a large extent devoid of gender attributes, serving women, *qua* women, are more vulnerable than their male counterparts: "But in certain ways the gender and sexuality of female slaves matters in the Odyssey [...] even if it is regularly to the slaves' disadvantage....the moral quality of the female slaves is measured by their sexual behavior, whereas the standard for male slaves is their action for or against their master."

260 E.g., Othonia and Hypodameia are two maids whom Penelope likes to have with her as attendants, Eurynome is the housekeeper, and Eurymedusa is Nausicaa's nurse.

261 On the way in which the *Odyssey* structures the legal and social status of the male and female servants, see Thalmann 1998, 22. Also see Olson 1992, 219.

leads to their violent silencing. At the same time, these two women servants illustrate the persistent efforts by women who risk their lives to exercise agency and autonomy.

Before proceeding, let me focus on the general representation of serving women and slaves in the *Odyssey*. Erich Auerbach's influential *Mimesis* is an interesting source in this context. Partly due to opening chapter, "The Scar of Odysseus," in which Eurycleia plays a leading role, the book has gained notable presence in Western culture.[262] In this chapter, Auerbach notes Homer's unique style, seemingly employing several general assumptions. About Eurycleia he writes:

> The housekeeper Euryclea [...] she is closely connected with their fate, she loves them and shares their interests and feelings. But she has no interests of her own, no feelings of her own; she has only the life and feelings of her master.[263]

Auerbach proceeds toward the following generalization: "In the Homeric poems life is enacted only among the ruling class."[264] On his analysis, the narrative concentrates on the struggles between various groups of "masters," whom Homer describes fully. On everything that happens beyond these conflicts, Auerbach notes "Nothing ever pushes up from below."[265]

Indeed, the description of the sayings and doings of the slaves and serving women always serves to advance the plot that focuses on men and women of the upper class. Throughout the *Odyssey* slaves and serving women almost never speak or conduct interactions among themselves.[266] Yet even though their affairs constitute a sideline to the plot, a close reading of the text gives rise, to use Auerbach's terms, to a series of discrepancies and troubling questions regarding the serving women. In effect, by shaping their characters, Homer is doing much more than advancing the plot of the major protagonists.

Let us begin with Eurycleia. Besides describing her as having been extremely loyal to the House of Odysseus throughout her life, the storyteller also hints that her conduct is the product of a life of subjugation; that the young girl sold into slavery became a trained and obedient old woman through a combination of fear and survival instinct.

---

262 Erich Auerbach, *Mimesis: The Representation of Reality in Western Literature*, trans. Willard R. Trask (Princeton, NJ: Princeton University Press, 2003) (hereinafter abbreviated as Auerbach 2003).
263 Auerbach 2003, 21.
264 Auerbach 2003, 21.
265 Auerbach 2003, 21.
266 See Thalmann 1998, 27.

As a child, Eurycleia was purchased by Laertes, Odysseus' father, who "Fearing the queen's anger" (*Odyssey* 1.493), elected to forgo his right to have sexual relations with her and assigned Eurycleia to other duties instead. She nursed Odysseus as a baby and child, and afterward also his son Telemachus, and she continues to vigilantly protect their interests even as adults. Accordingly, in the narrative Eurycleia performs various tasks to ensure Odysseus' successful return. She helps Telemachus set out on his search, concealing his departure from his mother; she locks the hall doors to prevent the suitors from escaping the slaughter. She clearly will do whatever is required in Odysseus and his son's service. The "scar scene" for which she is remembered most takes place when she is washing Odysseus' feet upon his return to his home disguised as a beggar. His identity is revealed to her when she sees the scar on his foot, which she recognizes after having treated the old injury in Odysseus' youth (*Odyssey* 19.386–504). Odysseus violently stifles her enthusiastic recognition. He grabs her by the throat and threatens her life:

> Quiet! Not a word to anyone in the house.
> Or else, I warn you – and I mean business too
> If a god beats down these brazen suitors at my hands,
> I will not spare you – my old nurse that you are
> When I kill the older women in my house (*Odyssey* 19.550–554)

There is a jarring discrepancy between Eurycleia's joyful recognition of her master and Odysseus' threat. Eurycleia promises to keep silent, but reveals her own trump card: it would be unwise of Odysseus to kill her because she is in possession of important information that she will divulge when he defeats the suitors:

> One more thing. Take it to heart, I tell you.
> If a god beats down these brazen suitors at your hands,
> I'll report in full on the women in your house:
> Who are disloyal to you, who are guiltless (*Odyssey* 19.559–562)

The male *Metis Syndrome* resonates throughout this scene. Even after decades of devoted service to him, Odysseus still mistrusts Eurycleia and believes that only a threat of death would ensure that she causes him no harm.[267] As to Eurycleia,

---

267 On Odysseus' suspicion toward her, which is essentially no different from the suspicion he feels toward every woman *qua* woman, including his wife Penelope, the paragon of ultra-devotion, Thalmann states, "Eurycleia's intimate knowledge of Odysseus's body and his history makes him vulnerable to her [...] And it seems to be as female, and not just as slave, that Odys-

the need to allay male suspicion and ensure male satisfaction with her services seems to be ingrained in her. Against this background, her actions make sense. It is difficult to imagine that she might be able to breaking free of the chains that bind her since early childhood. In contrast, the choices and actions of Melantho, who serves in the same household, are surprising. We are told that:

> Dolius was her father but Penelope brought her up;
> She treated her like her own child and gave her toys
> To cheer her heart. But despite that, her heart
> Felt nothing for all her mistress's anguish now.
> She was Eurymachus' lover, always slept with him (*Odyssey* 18.365–369)

As emerges from these lines, Melantho decides to shed the confines of her status. Together with her brother Melanthius, she chooses to join the suitors who challenge the household in which they both serve. Melanthius provides the best of the goats from Odysseus' herd for the suitors' banquets. He also joins in their festivities, basking in the favor shown him by their leader Eurymachus (*Odyssey* 17.257), who took Melanthius' attractive sister Melantho as a lover. Eleven other serving women also have intimate relations with the suitors.

In the case of Melantho, is this a freely made choice? Is it possible that her brother, who gambled on the victory of Eurymachus in the struggle between Telemachus and the suitors over control of the palace, enlisted her to help him gain a position of favor in the suitors' camp? In *The Penelopiad*, Atwood suggests that Penelope herself sent Melantho, her trusted protégée, and other serving women, to seduce and spy on the suitors.[268] Has Melantho chosen to couple with Eurymachus out of love or passion, or perhaps it was an opportunistic move to ensure her own future, in anticipation of his victory in the battle for the future control of the palace?

What were the motives of the remaining serving women? One possibility is that the suitors forced these low-status, unprotected girls to sleep with them. This possibility is supported by a conversation between Odysseus, disguised as a beggar, Telemachus, and the swineherd Eumaeus, in the course of which Odysseus repeats what he has learned of the suitors' scandalous acts:

---

seus does not fully trust her, for in the same way he does not confide in Penelope either" (Thalmann 1998, 28).

268 Atwood describes how Penelope enlists the serving women: "You must pretend to be in love with these men. If they think you have taken their side, they'll confide in you and we'll know their plans. It's one way of serving your master, and he'll be very pleased with you when he comes home" (Atwood 2005, 117).

> Men dragging the serving-women
> Through the noble house, exploiting them all, no shame,
> And the gushing wine swilled [...] (*Odyssey* 16.121–122)

Before killing the suitors, Odysseus also accuses them of having "ravished my serving women" (*Odyssey* 22.38). At the same time, however, the text repeatedly notes that the serving women "went tramping to their shame" (*Odyssey* 22.449). Doherty notes that the text intentionally repeats that the serving women freely chose to have sexual relations with the suitors.[269] Yet the text mentions both possibilities – rape or free choice – without ascribing any importance to deciding between them. Ultimately, the women's "guilt" or "innocence" is never determined, which only intensifies the moral outrage of their murder.

Odysseus orders his son to kill the women by the sword, but Telemachus decides to hang them from a ship's hawser, to add to their suffering and humiliation.[270] These women, it could be argued, serve as scapegoats, and their execution due to their sexual infidelity contrasts with the theme of Penelope's fidelity and diverts attention from the elements that create doubt regarding her fidelity.[271] On this view, the serving women are sacrificed on the altar of the patriarchy's interests, but also on the altar of the women belonging to the dominant class. Would such gynocide become impossible under the rule of law that emerged in Athens in the following generations, the seeds of which would be given renowned artistic expression in the *Oresteia?* Sadly, the answer appears to be negative. It is highly doubtful that a legal order whose first action is to acquit a confessed perpetrator of matricide will grant powerless low-class women protection that was absent in the age of the epics. Orestes' acquittal can be read as the victory of the patriarchy, which was able to expand and entrench partiality

---

269 Doherty 1995, 155.

270 For a review of the responses in the literary research to this move by Telemachus, including an interpretation that it proves the lad has the ability in principle to assume his place in due time as a worthy ruler, see Laurel Fulkerson, Epic Ways of Killing a Woman: Gender and Transgression in Odyssey 22.465–72," *The Classical Journal* 97.4 (2002): 335–350, 347 (hereinafter abbreviated as Fulkerson 2002).

271 See Fulkerson 2002, 347. Fulkerson writes: "Those deaths (perhaps deliberately) mirror the foreclosed discussion of Penelope's faithfulness. Just as the recognition between Penelope and Odysseus is displaced onto other characters, so too is the vexed question of Penelope's fidelity. The women, like the suitors, serve as scapegoats for anything improper that was done in Ithaca while Odysseus was away."

to male over female interests even where women of high status are concerned, and simultaneously to justify it legally.[272]

Thousands of years after the writing of the *Odyssey*, the failures of criminal justice continue to echo. In Atwood's *The Penelopiad*, the literary work that brings the murdered women back to life and gives them their day in court,[273] the women collectively say:

> we had no voice
> we had no name
> we had no choice
> we had one face
> one face the same
> we took the blame
> it was not fair
> but now we're here.[274]

But even in this imaginary domain the judicial procedure fails, as far as the murdered women are concerned. Atwood's all-male court manages to find legal justification for acquitting Odysseus of their murder, reverberating Orestes' acquittal of his mother's murder in the *Oresteia*.

To summarize, Melantho and the other serving women may have been raped, but the narrative leaves room for another possibility, namely that the twelve women attempted to take control of their sexuality and perhaps their lives in general. For a short period of time they were able to act with agency and break free of their gender and status bonds. Even if the epic allows them to do so, it imposes on them a gruesome punishment, which echoes Metis' fate. The epics are clear: disloyal women who imprudently flaunt their agency will be considered threatening to men and will pay with their lives.[275]

Athena

As noted by Wilson, Athena of the *Odyssey* is the prime mover of events:

---

272 For an assessment in a similar spirit of the law in Athens, see David Cohen, "The Theodicy of Aeschylus: Justice and Tyranny in the Oresteia," *Greece and Rome* 33.2 (1986): 129–141, 129.

273 Atwood 2005.

274 Atwood 2005, 195–196.

275 The death of the serving women, writes Doherty in a similar spirit, gives rise to a cautionary tale aimed at women: "[s]lave women like Penelope's handmaids are not addressed by the poem – except, perhaps, indirectly: for them the fate of Melantho and of the other 'bad' handmaids could serve as a cautionary tale" (Doherty 1995, 119).

The poem's plot is, of course, engineered by the wonderfully gender-fluid goddess Athena.[276]

This Athena is surrounded by many others Athenas, each a reflection of the changes in the way the goddess was perceived by those who passed on the stories about her from one generation to the next.[277] It could be argued that what underlies Hesiod's description of the myth is an intention to conceal Athena's link to her mother Metis, and Athena's threat to Zeus as the powerful patroness of mortal heroes.[278] By repeatedly underscoring the circumstances of her birth and that Zeus is her sole progenitor, Hesiod indeed emphasizes Athena's role, from the outset, as heiress to force and power that poses no threat to Zeus.[279]

To this narrow, instrumentalist characterization of Athena, which aligns with the warning against perfidious femininity embedded in the male *Metis Syndrome*, the *Odyssey* adds an interesting complexity. From the very first moments of her appearance in the storyline, a sense of tension ensues between Athena's loyalty to Zeus and her potential threat to Zeus' supremacy.[280] Athena is the first to bring up the matter of Odysseus, in the course of a gathering of the gods. Zeus remarks that men are responsible for the troubles that befall them, citing the bitter fate of Aegisthus who failed to heed the gods' warnings and thus was justly murdered by Orestes. With rhetorical wile, Athena tilts the conversation in a different direction, and ensnares Zeus by manipulatively using the idea he just mentioned: If, as Zeus says, it is befitting to punish those who have sinned, Athena argues, then it certainly is *not* befitting to punish Odysseus, who not only had not sinned but had given Zeus great satisfaction. Athena first speaks emotionally in what might be considered a stereotypical feminine mode of expression:

> But my heart breaks for Odysseus,
> that seasoned veteran cursed by fate so long (*Odyssey* 1.57–58)

Immediately, though, her rhetoric becomes demanding, and in it there is more than a trace of criticism of her father and his choices:

---

276 Wilson 2017.

277 For an instructive review of the history of the development of the use of Athena's character and the abundance of cultural contexts in which it appears, see Deacy 2008, 122–156.

278 For such argument, see Norman Brown's essay analyzing the various appearances and meanings of the myth of Athena's birth (Brown 1952, 135).

279 Hesiod mentions that Zeus swallowed Metis into his belly three times, and twice recites the circumstances of Athena's extraordinary birth. See *The Theogony* 886–900, 929–300.

280 For the list of ancient sources in which Athena is referenced as a potential threat to Zeus, see Deacy 2008, 122–156.

> Olympian Zeus,
> Have you no care for *him* in your lofty heart?
> Did he never win your favour with sacrifices
> Burned beside the ships on the broad plain of Troy?
> Why, Zeus, why so dead set against Odysseus? (*Odyssey* 1.72–75)

Zeus finds himself on the defensive. He denies not caring for Odysseus or having forgotten the sacrifices offered by him, and cites a constraint that justifies his nonintervention until now: Poseidon's objection. Nonetheless, despite the constraint, he succumbs to Athena's pressure, instructing the divine forum to decide on how to advance Odysseus' return home. Athena needs no advice from the others. She explains to them what will happen next: Hermes shall be dispatched to Calypso's island to command her to send Odysseus home, while Athena herself will go to Ithaca to help Odysseus' son prepare for his return. From here on, Athena conducts the campaign of Odysseus' return to Ithaca with cunning, determination, and brute force. She empowers Telemachus, addresses the public in Ithaca disguised as Mentor, reveals herself to Odysseus and together with him plans the confrontation with the suitors, aggravates the suitors' reactions, and actively uses her skills as a goddess of war. Throughout the plot Athena's power is never hidden; it is evident and demonstrated at every possible opportunity. Toward the end, Zeus himself acknowledges Athena's pulsating force. Before the final battle between Odysseus and his adversaries, Athena addresses him:

> Father, son of Cronus, our high and mighty king,
> Now let me ask you a question [...]
> Tell me the secrets hidden in your mind.
> Will you prolong the pain, the cruel fighting here
> Or hand down pacts of peace between both sides? (*Odyssey* 24.522–526)

To which Zeus replies:

> My child [...] why do you pry and probe me so intently? Come now,
> Wasn't the plan your own? You conceived it yourself:
> Odysseus should return and pay the traitors back.
> Do as your heart desires –
> But let me tell you how it should be done (*Odyssey* 24.527–532)

Zeus' reply unmasks Athena's request as pandering, perhaps even a manipulative gesture: in effect, Zeus is surprised that Athena thinks he might have a hidden agenda as she was the one who has managed the entire affair from the start. He supports her desire to carry out her strategy, but tells her that she should follow operational plans that he devises. His cooperation seems to stem from paternal acquiescence to Athena's agenda rather than from his acknowledgment of his daughter's superiority.

Athena of the *Odyssey* is described as free of inhibitions or concerns. As a female goddess, she is exempt from the need to be cautious or disguise her power, which is typical of the other female characters. Athena makes powerful use of the skills that had been quashed in her mother – sagacity, shrewd strategizing, and inventiveness – and combines them with the martial skills inherited from her father. She has great affection for male heroes, but she is not yet described as someone who has unequivocally chosen her masculine side. Clearly, her sympathy and commitment are given to men, especially Odysseus and Telemachus, yet she maintains significant communications with women. For example, she appears in Nausicaa's dreams and influences her conduct. She similarly maintains a channel of communication with Penelope, and influences her behavior by planting in her mind the idea of the weaving stratagem and the archery contest. She also enhances Penelope's beauty, and in general treats her favorably.

Alongside descriptions of her practical cunning (*metis*), sagacity and martial skills, Athena of the *Odyssey* also plays a role in promoting and entrenching the social order. She demonstrates a commitment to the operation of social institutions and proper conduct of political life. She tries to influence the assembly summoned by Telemachus in Ithaca, produces an assembly to help Odysseus in the land of the Phaeacians, and at the conclusion of the epic she witnesses the parties' agreements and alliance. Against this backdrop, it is only natural that Athena should later become the establisher and patroness of criminal justice, the instrument that preserves the social order. But for this development to occur, the later Athena was required to shed the gender fluidity that characterizes her in the *Odyssey*, and assume an unequivocal and uncompromising commitment to the male interest. Athena is uniquely suited for this role in view of her origins as a virgin detached from matters of sexuality and fertility, and as a motherless daughter committed solely to her father.

The moment she becomes the founder of criminal justice is when Aeschylus presents her on the Athenian stage in the *Oresteia*. It is then that Athena denies her feminine side, and harnesses the new social instrument that she is establishing – the rule of law – in service of men:

> For there is no mother who gave birth to me
> and I approve the male principle in all things and with all my heart –
> except in the matter of marriage, and am very much my father's child (*Eumenides* 736–738)

Athena makes this statement the heart of the *Oresteia*.[281] Orestes' acquittal of his mother's murder, primarily because the victim was a woman, becomes the primary representation of judicial action on which the rule of law is predicated. From its original demarcation by its patroness Athena, the rule of law is designed as a tool serving the superiority and privileged status of the patriarchal elite.[282]

In the *Odyssey*, however, this has not yet happened. The society described in the *Odyssey* is committed in a general way to a social order regularized by rules and conventions and to the principle of justice but is still far from endorsing the rigid framework of formal rule of law that would be elaborately sketched for the first time in the *Oresteia*, in a way that actually means female defeat in the struggle for equality.

In significant ways, Athena of the *Odyssey* is closer to the ideal of justice than Athena of tragedy, the founder of criminal justice. Homeric Athena does not conceal her impartiality toward Odysseus and Telemachus beneath the camouflage of general theories of male superiority. She acts in an independent, direct manner to promote the interests of her protégées. In contrast, Athena of the *Oresteia* establishes the rule of law and the complex judicial apparatus it entails, ostensibly to ensure equality before the law, but in fact champions inequality.

Conclusion

In *Poetics*, Aristotle writes that with respect to the artistic shaping of characters, appropriateness is important and "it is not appropriate in a female character to be manly, or clever."[283] It would seem that Homer, despite the great praise his work received from Aristotle, did not have a similar view in mind when he created the brave and wise female characters in the *Odyssey*.

---

281 Luban 1986, 303–304. According to Luban, the bluntness of the remarks Aeschylus allots to Athena's indicates that Aeschylus wanted to clearly and unequivocally assert that Athena tilts justice in favor of Orestes, as an expression of the view that the subjugation of women to men is an integral component of the social order.

282 Deacy 2008, 153–156. Against this background, it is interesting to note that in the feminist writing dealing with Athena's character there is a spirited debate between a view of the goddess as representing female power, versus a view of her as representing a femininity that harnesses itself to patriarchal interests and is damaging to women.

283 *The Poetics of Aristotle*, Butcher trans. 1902, 53.

The myth of Metis is central to the reading of the *Odyssey* proposed here. This myth represents both the female defeat in the primordial struggle for control, and the subsequent female refusal to capitulate, alongside ceaseless striving to change the oppressive situation. The *Odyssey*'s epic tale reflects this duality: the inferiority to which women are sentenced, and their refusal to surrender to it. The *Odyssey* tells us of queens, princesses, goddesses, and serving women who try and, in many cases, succeed in manipulating the social system and its customary rules.

In effect, the *Odyssey* is female driven. Calypso rescues Odysseus and fights to keep him with her, mounting a vigorous effort to put forward an argument of gender equality. Nausicaa promotes the possibility of choosing Odysseus as her husband – a naked stranger whose life she saved – contrary to all class conventions and rules. Helen, who by her own admission abandoned "my own child, my bridal bed, my husband too" (*Odyssey* 4.295), returns after the fall of Troy to her royal status as queen beside the cuckolded Menelaus, without paying any price for her sexual infidelity.[284] Penelope succeeds in rebuffing the suitors for years, defending her independence and interests, and inducing them to give her expensive gifts. When Odysseus returns, she decides how the resumption of their conjugality will proceed, and tests him in several ways. Even the serving women in Odysseus' household try to claim their own space of independent action, albeit unlike Helen, they pay for it with their lives. And then, of course, there is Athena. Athena of the epics is she who returns Odysseus to his home, and her shining power there perhaps alludes to a threat to Zeus' hegemony. She does it all without expressing the absolute commitment to men that is assumed by Athena the founder of criminal justice in the *Oresteia*, hundreds of years later.

The era of the epics – a pre-judicial era – is marked by the *Metis Syndrome*. The epic allows women some freedom of action, if its exercise is disguised, which requires sophistication and cunning. The social system affords some balance between the social and political environment centered on male will and interest, and between women's ability to surrender to the androcentric default option while promoting their own interests and desires. They are excluded from the public sphere. The male *Metis Syndrome* renders them always suspect of subver-

---

284 Doherty 1995, 59. As noted by Doherty, it seems that Helen's status as a daughter of Zeus exempts her from compliance with the norms that apply to other women. She is protected by some type of immunity and is not punished or harmed for her adultery. Helen thus differs from other women, regarding whom other standards are fully enforced, but nonetheless her minor but significant role in the *Odyssey*, as a powerful woman doing as she will in an androcentric universe, cannot be overlooked.

sion and disloyalty.[285] Nonetheless, the women in the *Odyssey* do not use the opportunities available to them to influence their own destiny.

The result is a complex dynamic of balances that leaves women, at least privileged women such as Penelope, Helen, Nausicaa, and Arete, greater space to maneuver compared to what they can expect in the future when the declared and fixed rule of law turns into another instrument of patriarchal society.

In that later time, the *Metis Syndrome*, which also represents female power and the need to hide it, will fade. The era of tragedy would decide clearly and sharply in favor of male superiority, to the constant service of which the freshly minted rule of law would be harnessed and committed. But this construction of the rule of law has not been formalized in the era of the epic.

The *Odyssey* marks the starting point of the conflict between the sexes, while the *Oresteia* marks the female defeat in that struggle, one of whose primary expressions concerns the nature that the rule of law will come to assume.[286] Clytemnestra, a woman who openly chooses to exercise brute power – or in other words, to act like a man – will pay with her life. Her death will give rise to the first court, which will absolve her son, the murderer, of any responsibility. In tragedy, a man's acquittal of a woman's murder, an acquittal based on the victim's being a woman, will turn into the generative narrative of what will henceforth be called "the rule of law."

In the pantheon of a new and feminine mythopeia, which by self-conscious and deliberate appropriation of ancient myths will shatter the oppressive patterns imprinted into human consciousness, an important place is reserved for Metis.

---

285 Cantarella 1987, 24–33.

286 Luban 1986, 300. As Luban proposes, following Engels, the *Oresteia* marks what can be called "the world historical defeat of the female sex." Friedrich Engels, *The Origin of the Family, Private Property and the State*, ed. Eleanor Bruke Leacock (New York: International Publishers, 1978/1972), 120. For a similarly pessimistic appreciation of the rule of law in Athens, see Cohen 1986, 129–141.

Coda

The quest of a mythic hero, as famously posited by Joseph Campbell, has universal features. One of them is the common outline of a plan: "Whether the hero be ridiculous or sublime, Greek or barbarian, gentile or Jew, his journey varies little in essential plan."[287] The basic plan almost always involves the return of a hero with a boon for the world: "The full round, the norm of the monomyth, requires that the hero shall now begin the labor of bringing the runes of wisdom [...] back into the kingdom of humanity, where the boon may rebound to the renewing of the community [...]."[288]

The societal benefits of the hero's return are the *raison d'etre* of the mythic journey, and, from the standpoint of the community, its ultimate justification.[289] My central aim here was to introduce one of the most valuable societal benefits pertaining to the Homeric heroes' quests, specifically the subtle, preliminary introduction to the justification of the rule of law that emerges from the *Iliad* and the *Odyssey* recited together, as a whole.

This initial appreciation of society's need for an order based on law is not celebrated within the Homeric narrative. Instead, it evolved gradually, and could perhaps be fully appreciated only in retrospective. Yet, once revealed, it gained perpetual relevance, becoming an integral component of the continuous reification of the notion of law, created and maintained by literature.

Both the *Iliad* and the *Odyssey* offer tentative notions of establishing lines of defense against uncontrolled wrath, cruelty and injustice that trap men and women in violence, killing and being killed, separated from their homes and families, doomed to sorrow, fear, grief, and violent death. Out of stories about the terrible toll of unharnessed force appears the inevitability as well as the feasibility and advantage of forming societal institutions against the fatal combination of power and unrestricted self-interest. The *Iliad* ends with a hastily led burial. The Trojans bury Hector, fearing "the Achaean combat troops would launch their attack before the time agreed" (*Iliad* 24.939–940). This ending reverberates the disaster-prone fate of a lawless society. The *Iliad* concludes with fear of betrayal, the certainty that agreements are easily and commonly breached, and the sheer terror of the impending annihilation of an entire community. However the mythic quest continues and comes to its end later, in the *Odyssey*, which concludes in a very different tone: "And Athena handed down her pacts of peace

---

287 Campbell, 2004, 35.
288 Campbell, 2004, 177.
289 Campbell, 2004, 177.

https://doi.org/10.1515/9783110766110-007

between both sides for all the years to come" (*Odyssey* 24.599 – 600). Admittedly, the peace is achieved after a bloody carnage and only because Athena made Odysseus' rivals forget their losses, but further violence is effectively prevented by this pact, a boon presented by the mythic hero to the entire community, and to both allies and foes, which will eventually blossom into the generative legal narrative presented in the *Oresteia* several centuries later.

The Homeric epics are an essential link in a chain of stories about the establishment of law. Indeed, as Bespaloff suggests, it is perhaps the great Greek lawmakers rather than the philosophers that are the true heirs to Homeric wisdom.[290] The epics assign a central role to divine power, but at the same time it underscores the responsibility of humans to tell a new story with law at its center. It is the task of humans to distill the idea of the rule of law from the stories recounting the arbitrariness of the gods and the uncontrolled violence of humans: "Law is altogether a human work [...] Concern for justice remains man's secret pride before the anarchy of the gods [...]."[291]

As would become clear over the course of generations, law is part of a constantly developing human endeavor, driven by both noble and evil intentions, with the power to do good or to harm and the ability to protect the social order and the capacity to destroy it. Still, as the paradigm *of law alongside literature* asserts, law is indispensable. The artistic works discussed here reveal the arbitrary-delusionary basis of the legal sphere, and at the same time re-establish the law as part of a tremendous human achievement. They delineate law one as of the focal accounts of human experience, an essential effort connected to the most sophisticated aspects of existence, marked by courage, vision, and achievement. Law is also deemed to produce mistakes, failures, and disappointments, yet it can never be abandoned. The continuous flow of *law alongside literature* supports the everlasting hope of bettering the law.

---

290 Bespaloff 2005, 97.
291 Bespaloff 2005, 97–98.

Quotations in Headings

https://doi.org/10.1515/9783110766110-008

Bibliography

Adkins, Arthur W. H, *Merit and Responsibility: A Study in Greek Values* (Oxford: Clarendon Press, 1960).

Adorno, Theodor W. and Max Horkheimer, *Dialectic of Enlightenment*, trans. John Cumming (London: Verso, 1997).

Aeschylus, *Agamemnon*, trans. Hugh Lloyd-Jones (Englewood Cliffs, NJ: Prentice-Hall, 1970).

Aeschylus, *The Eumenides*, trans. Hugh Lloyd-Jones (Englewood Cliffs, NJ: Prentice-Hall, 1970).

Aeschylus, *The Libation Bearers*, trans. Hugh Lloyd-Jones (Englewood Cliffs, NJ: Prentice-Hall, 1970).

Ahrensdorf, Peter J., *Homer on the Gods and Human Virtue: Creating the Foundations of Classical Civilization* (New York: Cambridge University Press, 2014).

Allen, Danielle S., "Law and Greek Tragedy," in *Cambridge Companion to Greek Law & Culture*, eds. David Cohen and Michael Gagarin (Cambridge: Cambridge University Press, 2005), 374–393.

Almog, Shulamit, "Literature alongside law as a contemporary paradigm," *Cultural Dynamics* 13.1 (2001): 53–65.

Almog, Shulamit, "From Sterne and Borges to Lost Storytellers: Cyberspace, Narrative, and Law," *Fordham Intellectual Property, Media & Entertainment Law Journal* 13.1 (2002): 1–34.

Almog, Shulamit, "Creating Representations of Justice in the Third Millennium: Legal Poetics in Digital Times," *Rutgers Computer & Technology Law Journal* 32.2. (2006): 183–245.

Almog, Shulamit, "Windows and 'Windows': Reflections on Law and Literature in the Digital Age," *University of Toronto Law Journal* 57.4 (2007): 755–780.

Almog, Shulamit, "From the Odyssey Onwards: Law's Long and Winding Road," *Law & Literature* 32.1 (2002): 47–74. doi: 10.1080/1535685X.2019.1613092

Amsterdam, Anthony G. and Jerome S. Bruner, *Minding the Law* (Cambridge, MA: Harvard University Press, 2000).

An Oresteia: Agamemnon by Aeschylus; Elektra by Sophocles; Orestes by Euripides. Trans. Anne Carson, 2009. New York: Farrar, Straus and Giroux.

Arad, Maya, *All about Abigail.* Ben Shemen: Modan / Xargol Books. (Hebrew)

Arieti, James A., "Achilles' Guilt," *The Classical Journal* 80.3 (1985): 193–203.

Aristodemou, Maria, "The Seduction of Mimesis: Theater as Woman and the Play of Difference and Excess in Aeschylus's 'Oresteia'," *Cardozo Studies in Law and Literature* 11.1 (1999): 1–33.

Aristodemou, Maria, *Law & Literature: Journeys from Her to Eternity* (Oxford: Oxford University Press, 2000).

Atwood, Margaret, *The Penelopiad* (Edinburgh: Canongate, 2005).

Auerbach, Erich, *Mimesis: The Representation of Reality in Western Literature*, trans. Willard R. Trask (New Jersey: Princeton University Press, 2003).

Aristotle, *The Poetics of Aristotle*, ed. and trans. Samuel Henry Butcher 3rd ed. (London; New York: Macmillan, 1902).

Bakhtin, Michael, *Speech Genres and Other Late Essays*, trans. Vern W. McGee, eds. Caryl Emerson and Michael Holquis (Austin: University of Texas Press, 1986).

https://doi.org/10.1515/9783110766110-009

Ball, Milner S., *Called by Stories: Biblical Sagas and Their Challenge for Law* (Durham, NC: Duke University Press, 2000).

Basset, Samuel Eliot, "Achilles' Treatment of Hector's Body," *Transaction and Proceeding of the American Philological Association* 64 (1933): 41–65.

Beard, Mary, "The Public Voice of Women," *Women's History Review* 24.5 (2015)): 809–818.

Benfey, Christopher, "Introduction: A tale of two Iliads," in *War and the Iliad*, eds. Simone Weil, Rachel Bespaloff, and Hermann Broch, trans. Mary McCarthy (New York, NY: New York Review Books, 2005), vii–xxiii.

Berry, David M. and Anders Fagerjord, *Digital Humanities: Knowledge and Critique in a Digital Age* (Cambridge, UK, Malden, MA: Polity, 2017).

Bespaloff, Rachel, "On the Iliad," in *War and the Iliad*, eds. Simone Weil, Rachel Bespaloff and Hermann Broch, trans. Mary McCarthy (New York, NY: New York Review Books, 2005), 39–100.

Binder, Guyora, and Robert Weisberg, *Literary Criticisms of Law* (Princeton, NJ: Princeton University Press, 2000).

Brooks, Peter, *Reading for the Plot: Design and Intention in Narrative* (New York: A.A. Knopf, 1984).

Brown, Calvin S., "Odysseus and Polyphemus: The Name and the Curse," *Comparative Literatures* 18.3 (1966): 193–202.

Brown, Norman O., "The Birth of Athena," *Transactions and Proceedings of the American Philological Association* 83 (1952): 130–143. doi:10.2307/283379

Butler, Samuel, *The Authoress of the Odyssey* (London: Longmans, Green, 1897).

Campbell, Joseph, *The Hero with a Thousand Faces* (Princeton, NJ: Princeton University Press, 2004).

Cantarella, Eva, *Pandora's Daughters: The Role and Status of Women in Greek and Roman Antiquity* (Baltimore: Johns Hopkins University Press, 1987).

Cantarella, Eva, "Private Revenge and Public Justice: The Settlement of Disputes in Homer's Iliad," *Punishment & Society* 3.4 (2001): 473–483.

Cavarero, Adriana, *In Spite of Plato: A Feminist Rewriting of Ancient Philosophy* (Cambridge: Polity Press, 1995).

Cohen, David, "The Theodicy of Aeschylus: Justice and Tyranny in the Oresteia," *Greece and Rome* 33.2 (1986): 129–141. doi:10.1017/S0017383500030278

Cohen, David, *Law, Violence, and Community in Classical Athens* (Cambridge, UK; New York: Cambridge University Press, 1995).

Cover, Robert M., *Narrative, Violence, and the Law: The Essays of Robert Cover*, eds. Martha Minow, Michael Ryan, and Austin Sarat (Ann Arbor: University of Michigan Press, 1992).

Culler, Jonathan, *Literary Theory: A Very Short Introduction* (Oxford; New York: Oxford University Press, 1997).

De Chiara-Quenzer, Deborah, "Aristotle, Achilles, Courage, and Moral Failure," in *Looking at Beauty to Kalon in Western Greece: Selected Essays from the 2018 Symposium on the Heritage of Western Greece*, eds. Heather L. Reid and Tony Leyh (Sioux City, IA: Parnassos Press, 2019), 189–202.

Deacy, Susan, *Athena* (London: Routledge, 2008).

Derrida, Jacques, "Force of Law: The 'Mystical Foundation of Authority' (Deconstruction and the Possibility of Justice)," *Cardozo Law Review* 11.5–6 (1990): 920–1045.

Detienne, Marcel, and Jean-Pierre Vernant, *Cunning Intelligence in Greek Culture and Society*, trans. Janet Lloyd (Chicago; London: University of Chicago Press, 1991).

Doherty, Lillian Eileen, *Siren Songs: Gender, Audiences, and Narrators in the Odyssey* (Ann Arbor: University of Michigan Press, 1995).

Dolmage, Jay, "Metis, Mêtis, Mestiza, Medusa: Rhetorical Bodies across Rhetorical Traditions," *Rhetoric Review* 28.1 (2009): 1.

Engel, David M., "Origin Myths: Narratives of Authority, Resistance, Disability, and Law," *Law & Society Review* 27.4 (1993): 785–826.

Engels, Friedrich, *The Origin of the Family, Private Property and the State*, ed. Eleanor Bruke Leacock (New York: International Publishers, 1978/1972).

Euripides. *Iphigenia in Aulis*, trans. Nicholas Rudall (Chicago: Ivan R. Dee, 1997).

Felson Robin, Nancy, *Regarding Penelope: From Character to Poetics* (Princeton, NJ: Princeton University Press, 1994).

Finkelberg, Margalit, *Homer* (Tel Aviv: The *Haim Rubin* Tel Aviv University Press, 2014). (Hebrew)

Finley, Moses I., *The World of Odysseus* (Harmondsworth: Penguin, 1972).

Friedrich, Rainer, "Zeus and the Phaeacians: Odyssey 13.158," *The American Journal of Philology* 110.3 (1989): 395–399.

Fulkerson, Laurel, "Epic Ways of Killing a Woman: Gender and Transgression in Odyssey 22.465–72," *The Classical Journal* 97.4 (2002): 335–350.

Gagarin, Michael, *Early Greek Law* (Berkeley, CA: University of California Press, 1986).

Gagarin, Michael, "Morality in Homer," *Classical Philology* 82.4 (1987): 285–306.

Gera, Judit, "The Voice of Circe," in *das rechte Maß getroffen*, eds. Ernő Kulcsár Szabó, Károly Manherz, and Magdolna Orosz (PLACE: Eötvös-Loránd Universität, 2004), 215–223.

Goldhill, Simon, *Aeschylus, the Oresteia*, 2nd ed. (Cambridge, UK; New York: Cambridge University Press, 2004).

Greek Tragedies 3: Aeschylus: The Eumenides; Sophocles: Philoctetes, Oedipus at Colonus; Euripides: The Bacchae, Alcestis, trans. Richmond Lattimore, eds. Mark Griffith, Glen W. Most, David Grene, and Richmond Lattimore (Chicago: University of Chicago Press, 2013).

Grethlein, Jonas, "Homeric Motivation and Modern Narratology: The Case of Penelope," *The Cambridge Classical Journal* 64 (2018): 70–90. doi:10.1017/S1750270517000136

Griffin, Jasper, *Homer on Life and Death* (Oxford: Clarendon Press, 1980).

Griffin, Jasper, *Homer, The Odyssey*, 2nd ed. (Cambridge: Cambridge University Press, 2004).

Gross, Nicolas P., "Nausicaa: A Feminine Threat," *The Classical World* 69.5 (1976): 311–317. doi:10.2307/4348437.

Guthrie, William K. C., *The Greeks and their Gods* (Boston: Beacon Press, 1955).

Harris, Edward Monroe, Delfim Ferreira Leao and P.J. Rhodes (eds.), *Law and Drama in Ancient Greece* (London: Bristol Classical Press, Bloomsbury Academic, 2012).

Hartmann, Anna-Maria, "An Undemocratic Turn?" *The Cambridge Quarterly* 47.3 (2018): 272–279.

Head, Barclay Vincent, *Historia Numorum: A Manual of Greek Numismatics* (Oxford: Clarendon Press, 1911).

Herodotus, *The Histories*, trans. Robin Waterfield (Oxford, UK: Oxford University Press, 1998).

Hesiod, *The Works and Days: Theogony. The Shield of Herakles*, trans. Richmond Lattimore (Ann Arbor: University of Michigan Press, 1959)

Hölkeskamp, Karl J., "Arbitrators, Lawgivers and the 'Codification of Law' in Archaic Greece: Problems and Perspectives," *Metis. Anthropologie des mondes anciens* 7 (1992): 49–81.

Holman, C. Hugh, and William Harmon, *A Handbook to Literature*, 6th ed. (New York: Macmillan, 1992).

Homer and Hesiod, "The Theogony," in *Hesiod, The Homeric Hymns, and Homerica* [1914], ed. and trans. Hugh G. Evelyn-White. Project Gutenberg (2008). https://www.gutenberg.org/files/348/348-h/348-h.htm

Homer, *The Odyssey*, trans. Robert Fagles (London: The Folio Society, 2001).

Homer, *The Iliad of Homer* [1951], trans. Richmond Lattimore (Chicago: University of Chicago Press, 1984).

Homer, *The Odyssey of Homer* [1965], trans. Richmond Lattimore (New York: Harper & Row, 1968).

Homer, *The Iliad*, trans. Robert Fagles (London: The Folio Society, 2001).

Horace, *Ars Poetica. Poetry Foundation* (website). (Adapted from translations by C. Smart and E. H. Blakeney, *Horace on the Art of Poetry* [London: Scholartis Press, 1928].) https://www.poetryfoundation.org/articles/69381/ars-poetica

Jacobs, Amber, "Towards a Structural Theory of Matricide: Psychoanalysis, the Oresteia and the Maternal Prohibition," *Women: A Cultural Review* 15.1 (2004): 19–34.

Jones, Lindsay and Gale Group, *Encyclopedia of Religion*, 2nd ed. (Detroit: Macmillan Reference, 2005).

Kass, Amy, "The Homecoming of Penelope: On Friendship in Homer's Odyssey," trans. Ido Hevroni, *Tochen Velnyanim* January 14, www.shalem.ac.il/content-channel/the-homecoming-of-penelope/ (Hebrew)

Katz, Marylin A., *Penelope's Renown: Meaning and Indeterminacy in the Odyssey* (Princeton, NJ: Princeton University Press, 2014).

Klein, Renate, *Surrogacy: A Human Rights Violation* (North Melbourne, Vic.: Spinifex Press, 2017).

Knox, Bernard, "Introduction to The Iliad," in *The Iliad*, trans. Robert Fagles (London: The Folio Society, 1996).

Kuhns, Richard, *The House, the City, and the Judge: the growth of moral awareness in the Oresteia* (Indianapolis: Bobbs-Merrill, 1962).

Lloyd-Jones, Hugh, *The Justice of Zeus* (Berkeley: University of California Press, 1983).

Louden, Bruce, "An Extended Narrative Pattern in the Odyssey," *Greek, Roman and Byzantine Studies* 34. (1993): 5–33. http://search.proquest.com/docview/229170662/.

Luban, David, "Some Greek Trials: Order and Justice in Homer, Hesiod, Aeschylus and Plato," *Tennessee Law Review* 54.2 (1986): 297–311.

Luban, David, *Legal Modernism* (Ann Arbor: University of Michigan Press, 1997).

MacLachlan, Bonnie, *Women in Ancient Greece: A Sourcebook* (London: Continuum, 2012).

Malkin, Irad, *The Returns of Odysseus: Colonization and Ethnicity* (Berkeley: University of California Press, 1998).

Marshall, C. W., "Casting the Oresteia," *The Classical Journal* 98.3 (2003): 257–274.

Mason, Wyatt, "The First Woman to Translate the 'Odyssey' into English," (New York) *The New York. Times Magazine* (November 2, 2017). https://www.nytimes.com/2017/11/02/magazine/the-first-woman-to-translate-the-odyssey-into-english.html

Mazon, Paul, Paul Collart, Pierre Chantraine, and René Langumier, *Introduction à l'Iliade* (Paris: Belles Lettres, 1943).

Miller, Madeline, *Circe* (New York, NY: Little, Brown and Company, 2018a).

Miller, Madeline, "Restoring Power to The Women of Ancient Myth," *Literary Hub* (website) April 11, 2018b. lithub.com/restoring-power-to-the-women-of-ancient-myth

Mishna, *Ethics of the Fathers* (Pirkei Avot), 3:15. (Hebrew)

Morrison, James V., "Kerostasia, The Dictates of Fate, and the Will of Zeus in the Iliad," *Arethusa* 30.2 (1997): 276–296.

Muellner, Leonard Charles, *The Anger of Achilles: 'Menis' in Greek Epic* (Ithaca, NY: Cornell University Press, 1996).

Murnaghan, Sheila, "Penelope's Agnoia: Knowledge, Power, and Gender in the Odyssey," in *Oxford Readings in Classical Studies: Homer's Odyssey*, ed. Lillian E. Doherty (Oxford: Oxford University Press, 2009), 231–244.

Nagler, Michael N., "Penelope's Male Hand: Gender and Violence in the Odyssey," *Colby Quarterly* 29.3 (1993): 241–257. https://digitalcommons.colby.edu/cq/vol29/iss3/7.

Neils, Jenifer, "Les Femmes Fatales: Skylla and the Sirens in Greek Art," in *The Distaff Side: Representing the Female in Homer's Odyssey*, ed. Beth Cohen (New York: Oxford University Press, 1995), 175–184.

Nietzsche, Friedrich Wilhelm, *The Birth of Tragedy* [1872], trans. Smith Douglas (Oxford; New York: Oxford University Press, 2000).

Nimis, Steve, "The Language of Achilles: Construction vs. Representation," *The Classical World* 79 (1986): 217–225.

Olson, S. Douglas, "Servants' Suggestions in Homer's Odyssey," *The Classical Journal* 87.3 (1992): 219–227.

Ostwald, Martin, *From Popular Sovereignty to the Sovereignty of Law: Law, Society, and Politics in Fifth-Century Athens* (Berkeley: University of California Press, 1986).

Parry, Adam, "The Language of Achilles," *Transactions and Proceedings of the American Philological Association* 87 (1956): 1–7.

Partington, Charles Frederick, *The British Cyclopedia of Biography: Containing the Lives of Distinguished Men of All Ages and Countries, with Portraits, Residences, Autographs, and Monuments* (London: Wm. S. Orr and Co., Amen Corner, Paternoster Row, 1838).

Pellikaan-Engel, Maja, "Calypso's Recipe: On Biased Traditions in Philosophy," *Western Libraries* (website) June 26, 2010. https://ir.lib.uwo.ca/iaph/June26/Presentations/8/.

Peradotto, John, *Man in the Middle Voice: Name and Narration in the Odyssey* (Princeton, NJ: Princeton University Press, 1990).

Plato. *Republic*. 332d-335c

Pomeroy, Sarah B., *Goddesses, Whores, Wives, And Slaves: Women in Classical Antiquity* (New York: Knopf Doubleday Publishing Group, 2011).

Pushkin, Alexander Sergeevich, *The Poems, Prose, and Plays of Alexander Pushkin*, trans. Avrahm Yarmilinsky (New York: The Modern Library, 1943).

Puttenham, George, *The Art of English Poesy*, eds. Frank Whigham and Wayne A. Rebhorn (Ithaca; London: Cornell University Press, 2007).

Redfield, James M, *Nature and Culture in the Iliad: The Tragedy of Hector* (Durham: Duke University Press, 1994).

Reeves, John D., "The Cause of the Trojan War: A Forgotten Myth Revived," *The Classical Journal* 61.5 (1966): 211–214.

Reiber, Robert W., *Freud on Interpretation: The Ancient Magical Egyptian and Jewish Traditions* (New York: Springer, 2012).

Richlin, Amy, *Zeus and Metis: Foucault, Feminism, Classics* (Lubbock, TX: Texas Tech University Press, 1991).

Rimmon-Kenan, Shlomit, *Narrative Fiction: Contemporary Poetics* (London: Routledge, 2003).

Roemer, Michael, *Telling Stories: Postmodernism and the Invalidation of Traditional Narrative* (Lanham, MD: Rowman & Littlefield, 1995).

Rose, Peter W., *"Class Ambivalence in the "Odyssey," Historia: Zeitschrift für Alte Geschichte* 24.2 (1975): 129–149.

Rowan Beye, Charles, *The Iliad, the Odyssey, and the Epic Tradition* (Garden City, NY: Doubleday, 1966).

Schlink, Bernard, *The Reader*, trans. Carol Brown Janeway (New York: Vintage, 2001), 182.

Segal, Charles, "Circean Temptations: Homer, Vergil, Ovid," *Transactions and Proceedings of the American Philological Association* 99 (1968): 419–442.

Segal, Charles, "Divine Justice in the Odyssey: Poseidon, Cyclops, and Helios," *The American Journal of Philology* 113.4 (1992): 489–518.

Shapiro, H. A., "Coming of Age in Phaiakia: The Meeting of Odysseus and Nausicaa," in *The Distaff Side: Representing the Female in Homer's Odyssey*, ed. Beth Cohen (New York: Oxford University Press, 1995), 155–164.

Skempis, Marios and Ioannis Ziogas, "Arete's Words: Etymology, Ehoie-Poetry and Gendered Narrative in the Odyssey," in *Narratology and Interpretation*, eds. Jonas Grethlein and Antonios Rengakos (Berlin: De Gruyter, 2009), 213–240.

Slatkin, Laura, *The Power of Thetis: Allusion and Interpretation in the Iliad* (Berkeley: University of California Press, 1991).

Stehle, Eva, "Sappho's Gaze: Fantasies of a Goddess and Young Man," in *Reading Sappho: Contemporary Approaches*, ed. Ellen Green (Berkeley, CA: University of California Press, 1996). 193–225.

Stehle, Eva, *Performance and Gender in Ancient Greece: Nondramatic Poetry in Its Setting* (Princeton, NJ: Princeton University Press, 1997).

Stern, Simon, "Literary Analysis of Law," in *The Oxford Handbook of Legal History*, eds. Markus D. Dubber and Christopher L. Tomlins (Oxford: Oxford University Press, 2018), 63–78.

Strauss-Clay, Jenny, *The Wrath of Athena: Gods and Men in the Odyssey* (Princeton, NJ: Princeton University Press, 1983).

Strauss-Clay, Jenny, "The Anger of Achilles: 'Mēnis' in Greek Epic (Book Review)," *The American Journal of Philology* 118.4 (1997): 631–634.

Taplin, Oliver, *Homeric Sounding: The Shaping of the Iliad* (Oxford: Clarendon Press, 1992).

Thalmann, William G., "Female Slaves in the Odyssey," in *Women and Slaves in Greco-Roman Culture*, eds. Sandra R. Joshel and Sheila Murnaghan (London: Routledge, 1998), 22–34.

Vernant, Jean-Pierre and Pierre Vidal-Naquet, *Myth and Tragedy in Ancient Greece*, trans. Janet Loyd (Sussex: Harvester Press, 1981).

Weil, Simone, "The Iliad, or the Poem of Force," in *War and the Iliad*, eds. Simone Weil, Rachel Bespaloff, and Hermann Broch, trans. Mary McCarthy (New York, NY: New York Review Books, 2005), 1–37.

West, Martin Litchfield, *The Making of the Odyssey* (Oxford; New York: Oxford University Press, 2014).

Westbrook, Raymond, "The Trial Scene in the Iliad," *Harvard Studies in Classical Philology* 94 (1992): 53–76.

White, James B, *The Legal Imagination: Studies in the Nature of Legal Thought and Expression* (Boston: Little, Brown, 1973).

Whitman, Cedric Hubbell, *Homer and the Heroic Tradition* (Cambridge, MA: Harvard University Press, 1958).

Whittaker, Helene, "The Status of Arete in the Phaeacian Episode of the Odyssey," *Symbolae Osloenses* 74.1 (1999/2008): 140–50. doi:10.1080/00397679908590959.

Williams, Glanville, "Language and the Law," *Law Quarterly Review* 61 (1945): 71–86.

Wilson, Emily, "A Translator's Reckoning with the Women of the Odyssey," *New Yorker*, December 8, 2017. https://www.newyorker.com/books/page-turner/a-translators-reckoning-with-the-women-of-the-odyssey

Wilson, John R, "Eris in Euripides," *Greece and Rome* 26.1 (1979): 7–20.

Worman, Nancy, "Reflection: Achilles and Homer's Iliad," in *Moral Motivation: A History*, ed. Iakovos Vasiliou (New York, NY: Oxford University Press, 2016), 39–43.

Zanghellini, Aleardo, "The Foundations of the Rule of Law," *Yale Journal of Law & the Humanities* 28.2 (2016): 213–240.

Zeitlin, Froma I., *Playing the Other: Gender and Society in Classical Greek Literature* (Chicago: University of Chicago Press, 1996).

Index

https://doi.org/10.1515/9783110766110-010

www.ingramcontent.com/pod-product-compliance
Lightning Source LLC
Chambersburg PA
CBHW031239260626
47169CB00007B/2377